PRAISE FOR
ALL THE FEELS

As the dad of four amazing daughters, *All the Feels for Teens* is truly a godsend. Elizabeth's book is winsome, witty, and delightfully practical. Against a beautiful gospel backdrop, she shows teen girls how God wonderfully designed their whole being—including their emotions—for his glory, their good, and the blessing of others. I'm definitely giving this book to my teens. (BTW, it even made a fortysomething dad LOL . . . JSYK.)

JOSHUA COOLEY
New York Times bestselling author whose books include *Creator, Father, King: A One Year Journey with God*; *The One Year Devotions with Jesus*; and *Heroes of the Bible Devotional*

A must-read for teens—and their parents! Elizabeth Laing Thompson is like the encouraging friend every teen needs in her life. In *All the Feels for Teens*, she will make you laugh, sit with you while you cry, and have you nodding in understanding, all while consistently pointing you to the God who not only understands your feelings but loves and adores you more than you can fathom. *All the Feels for Teens* is the right book for right now.

JENNIFER MARSHALL BLEAKLEY
Author of *Joey* and *Pawverbs*

I really liked this book. It helped me learn that I don't have to be scared of my feelings, and it taught me how to feel more in control of them and how to take them to God. I like Mrs. Thompson's writing style, and I think most teenagers will find this book very helpful.

ELLA BLEAKLEY, AGE 14

This book is phenomenal. I found myself relating to every chapter in some way, and I can honestly say that I understand myself better (and understand who God says I am better) after reading this book. Between the personal stories backed by Scripture and the moments of self-reflection, *All the Feels for Teens* has allowed me to truly understand my emotions. This book is full of laughs, but it's also full of relatable moments. No matter what type of feeler you are, it will help you to understand what your emotions mean and what God has to say about them.

GABRIELLA, AGE 17

All the Feels for Teens is an incredible book that changed how I view my emotions in my walk with the Lord. Every story and Scripture reference opened up a whole new world to me—one where God wants us to come to him with our emotions rather than push them down. This book will change the way you pray, read your Bible, and just live your life. The knowledge that God cares about your emotions will set you free.

ISABELLE, AGE 15

All the Feels for Teens is an awe-inspiring book, full of laughs and encouraging stories backed by Scripture. It helped me understand my emotions and how I process things. It helped me see myself as the beautifully imperfect creation God made me to be. No matter what kind of feeler you are, this book will change your perspective on emotions.

REBEKAH, AGE 15

All the Feels for Teens is an extremely useful tool for self-growth and understanding others better. Full of practical tips and prompts that encourage self-reflection, this book reminds us that emotions are special gifts that allow us to live fuller lives, but they don't have to rule over us. Using lessons continually supported by Scripture and an engaging writing style, Elizabeth teaches us how to handle and understand our emotions in a godly way, without underestimating their complexity or depth.

ARIANA, AGE 16

ALL THE FEELS FOR TEENS

THE GOOD, THE NOT-SO-GOOD,

ALL THE FEELS
FOR TEENS

AND THE UTTERLY CONFUSING

**ELIZABETH
LAING THOMPSON**

wander™
An imprint of
Tyndale House
Publishers

Visit Tyndale online at tyndale.com.

Visit the author online at ElizabethLaingThompson.com.

TYNDALE and Tyndale's quill logo are registered trademarks of Tyndale House Ministries. *Wander* and the Wander logo are trademarks of Tyndale House Ministries. Wander is an imprint of Tyndale House Publishers, Carol Stream, Illinois.

Designed by Libby Dykstra

Edited by Stephanie Rische

Published in association with the literary agency of Kirkland Media Management, P.O. Box 1539, Liberty, TX, 77575.

For information about special discounts for bulk purchases, please contact Tyndale House Publishers at csresponse@tyndale.com, or call 1-855-277-9400.

Library of Congress Cataloging-in-Publication Data

Names: Thompson, Elizabeth Laing, author.
Title: All the feels for teens : the good, the not-so-good, and the utterly
  confusing / Elizabeth Laing Thompson.
Description: Carol Stream, Illinois : Tyndale House Publishers, [2021]
Identifiers: LCCN 2021006461 (print) | LCCN 2021006462 (ebook) | ISBN
  9781496451071 (trade paperback) | ISBN 9781496451088 (kindle edition) |
  ISBN 9781496451095 (epub) | ISBN 9781496451101 (epub)
Subjects: LCSH: Teenage girls—Religious life. | Christian
  teenagers—Religious life. | Emotions in adolescence—Religious
  aspects—Christianity.
Classification: LCC BV4551.3 .T53 2021 (print) | LCC BV4551.3 (ebook) |
  DDC 248.8/33—dc23
LC record available at https://lccn.loc.gov/2021006461
LC ebook record available at https://lccn.loc.gov/2021006462

Printed in the United States of America

27	26	25	24	23	22	21
7	6	5	4	3	2	1

For Cassidy, Blake, Avery, and Sawyer:
with more love than words can hold

CONTENTS

ALL THE FEELS, ALL THE TIME

I still remember the first time I read the phrase *all the feels*. My heart gave a little hiccup and I laughed to myself. *All the feels? Welcome to my world.*

My big feelings made their dramatic appearance early in life—just wait till I tell you about the time I cried so hard I got my dad out of a speeding ticket!—but they hit new levels of intensity in middle school and high school. Maybe you know what I'm talking about: joy ballooning in your chest till you think your heart might pop, worry weighing down your soul till you forget how to smile, excitement consuming your thoughts till your brain is a blender.

Step into a classic example of how my feelings worked in high school. (Who knows—maybe this conversation will feel familiar to you . . .)

* * *

I barge through the front door, kick off my running shoes, and slouch into the kitchen, heaving out my frustration in angry huffs.

Mom stands at the counter, chopping carrots into tiny orange cubes. She raises an eyebrow. "That bad, huh?"

"Worse." I fling the refrigerator door open and lean inside, wishing the cool air could cool off my feelings.

"What happened?" Mom asks.

I grab a yogurt out of the fridge and shut the door so hard the jelly jars clink inside. "Well, I couldn't keep up with the varsity runners at cross-country practice—again." I yank off the yogurt lid, splattering pink yogurt slime all over the kitchen island.

Mom winces and reaches for a paper towel.

"It's not fair," I say, grabbing a spoon and stirring so hard a wet strawberry sloshes over the rim. "The varsity girls are all laughing and messing around, like, *la-di-da, running is easy*—and there I am, killing myself to keep up. But ever since I got sick, I just can't." I shove yogurt into my mouth and discover how hard it is to eat when you're trying not to cry.

"Oh, honey, it's not your fault you got sick. Besides," she says, turning to dump the carrots into a pot, "maybe God just gave those other girls really good running genes."

Anger flares inside, a hot streak that burns. "Well, if that's true, that makes it worse. That means God made me slow on purpose! That's so"—I choke back the word *mean*, because I'm pretty sure it's a sin to call God *mean*—"unfair." Even as the word leaves my mouth, I feel the twist of guilt inside. Mom presses her lips together. I can tell she wants to correct me, but she's holding back.

"Sorry," I mumble, shoving more yogurt into my mouth. *But I still feel that way.*

2

"Well, how was your math test?" Mom asks. I see what she's doing, trying to distract me, but I am determined to be miserable.

"Horrible."

"Really?" Mom's eyebrows shoot up. "Usually you—"

"I know," I moan. More shame weighing me down inside, like I just ate bricks instead of yogurt. I picture the homework assignments I've been letting slide, thinking I didn't need the practice. "I'm falling apart."

To her eternal credit, Mom doesn't push for more information. She doesn't ask why I did badly on the test or heap more guilt on me. She starts pulling plates from cabinets and setting the dinner table. I don't offer to help; I just stand there staring at my yogurt, thinking how the strawberry blobs look like pieces of my heart, cut up and mashed and stirred around.

Suddenly Mom speaks again, sounding chipper. "Hey, it's Thursday! Don't you have a phone date with Jack tonight? That always makes you feel better." She wiggles her eyebrows happily . . . hopefully.

I throw my head back. "Ughhhhh," I groan at the ceiling.

Mom's hopeful smile wilts. "Oh. I thought you'd be excited."

"Last week his friend was over, and they put me on speaker and spent the whole time making stupid jokes. It was like I wasn't even on the phone—I could have hung up and they never would have noticed."

"Well, have you told him how it makes you feel when he does that?"

"No. How can I say anything with Captain Dunderhead, his annoying friend, listening in the whole time?"

Mom's lips flatten into a line, and she turns to the sink; I see her shoulders rise and fall in a sigh. I slump onto the counter and bury my face in my arms. My voice is muffled, and I'm glad, because my words are awful. "Lately I feel like God doesn't care about my life. Sometimes I think he doesn't *want* me to be happy."

I wait for Mom to object, say something comforting, but there's only silence. I peek one eye up at her. "I'm horrible for saying that. And the Captain Dunderhead thing was mean. And now you're mad at me."

"I'm not mad at you." Mom spins back around to look at me, strangling a dish towel in her hands. "I just wish—I wish you weren't so negative about everything. You won't let anyone help you."

"That's not true," I mutter, but my words sound weak even to my own ears. "You help me." I push up onto my elbows.

Mom tilts her head down and gives me a look.

"Please don't be mad," I beg, feeling tears sting the backs of my eyes. "I can't have you mad at me on top of the Worst Day Ever. That would take it to even more epic levels of worst-ness."

Mom takes a deep breath. "I'm not mad, I'm just—I feel helpless. All you do is vent, and you don't really listen."

"I listen," I sniff.

The look again. I never knew eyebrows could be sarcastic.

"I'm listening now," I say, crossing my arms.

"I want you to know that all this"—she waves her hands in circles—"is just temporary. It's just feelings." When I make a noise of protest, she puts her palms up. "I'm not saying it isn't real. It's just not as bad as you're making it. You have a good life! You love God, and God loves you, and even if you're not running varsity or acing math, you can still be happy."

I shrug, trying to hear her, trying not to feel like the whole world is falling apart and God is against me and life is going to stink forever and ever.

"How about you go pray for a few minutes and then come down for dinner?" Mom finally says.

"Okay." I don't say what I'm thinking: *God feels far away right now.* I want to feel close, but when I'm like this, I'm not so sure God wants to hear from me. But out loud I say, "I'll try."

WHO'S IN CHARGE HERE?

Welcome to an inside look at my angsty teen years. Talk about all the feels, all the time. Does any of this sound—or maybe I should say *feel*—familiar?

If you ask any of your friends what their number one problem is in life, they might mention insecurity, anxiety, boys, school stress, friend problems, family issues, or worries about college and the future. Or they might mention depression or bullying or body-image concerns. But guess what all those problems have in common? They all deal with *feelings.*

If you're anything like me, some days your feelings fluctuate so dramatically you almost get whiplash. You can go from feeling giddy to anxious to insecure to in love—*oops, wait, just kidding, not in love at all; what was I thinking?*—to chill to stressed to ecstatic to depressed to in love with God to *meh* about God to needing your parents to wishing you could move out of your parents' house forever, all in a span of hours . . . sometimes minutes.

During middle and high school, most days I felt like my emotions were controlling me rather than the other way around. I *wanted* to be happy and at peace, I *wanted* to feel close to God and be a strong Christian, I *wanted* to be an unselfish daughter and sister and friend . . . but it often felt like my feelings were getting in the way, making me do and say things I didn't want to do and say. Sometimes I felt out of control, overwhelmed, and frustrated. I felt stuck. I had this picture in my mind of the kind of Christian—and person—I wanted to be, but the real me didn't always match that picture. I wanted to be different, to *feel* different, but I didn't know how.

There's good news for those of us who love God and seek to follow his ways. You might be surprised to hear this, but the Bible has a lot to say about our feelings. It tells us which feelings are godly and good for us, and it even gives us ideas for how to encourage those feelings to grow. The Bible also tells us which emotions we need to watch out for—which ones can hurt us if they get out of control—and gives us ideas for how we can limit or avoid them. The Bible can help us learn how to work on our feelings—to take charge of them, instead of letting them push us around.

I know what you're thinking: *Take charge of my feelings? What does that even mean? We can't do anything to change our feelings. Feelings are just . . . there. We don't have any control over what we feel, when we feel it, and how strongly we feel it . . . right?*

Actually, believe it or not, you and I have the chance to take charge of our emotions. We can learn how to keep our feelings from jerking us around all the time.

In the chapters to come, I can't wait to introduce you to some of the Scriptures and strategies that kept me going through high school. (Truth? They keep me going even now!) The more I've gotten to know my Bible, the more I've realized that God has something to say about *every* imaginable emotion. No matter what we feel, God understands, and he has put his counsel in his Word to help us. His guidance can transform the way we handle our feelings—and the way we feel from day to day.

IN GOD'S IMAGE

Did you know that our God is emotional too? He's not just some terrifying Judge in the Sky, peering down on the planet from his ginormous wooden bench, waiting to bang his gavel and toss us in spiritual jail when we mess up. Far from it! Our God is passionate and compassionate. Like us, he mourns; like us, he rejoices; like

What Does God Say about Emotions?

Sometimes God wants us to feel certain emotions—and sometimes he doesn't. Thankfully, the Bible helps us tell the difference. Write your answers below, including Bible verses that support your conclusion.

GOD WANTS US TO FEEL THIS EMOTION . . .	Always	Sometimes	Rarely	Never	SCRIPTURE THAT EXPLAINS YOUR ANSWER
Joy					
Fear					
Pride					
Humility					
Confidence					
Anger					

Tip: If you get stuck, try looking up these verses. You may find that some of these emotions are complicated—sometimes God wants us to feel them, and sometimes he doesn't! This isn't about right and wrong; it's about thinking through our emotions, and about the heart.

Psalm 71:5	Galatians 6:4	Philippians 2:3-4
Psalm 118:6	Ephesians 4:2	1 Thessalonians 5:16-18
Proverbs 1:7	Ephesians 4:26	1 John 4:18
Proverbs 15:18		
Proverbs 16:18		
Mark 3:5		

us, he feels all the feels. After all, he *invented* feelings. Take a look at this description of God the Father:

> As high as the heavens are above the earth,
>   so great is his love for those who fear him;
> as far as the east is from the west,
>   so far has he removed our transgressions from us.
>
> As a father has compassion on his children,
>   so the LORD has compassion on those who fear him.
>
> PSALM 103:11-13

God loves wild and big just like we do! And check out that line near the end: "As a father has compassion on his children, so the LORD has compassion on those who fear him." Do you grasp what a wondrous, mind-blowing truth that is? Almighty God, Maker of heaven and earth, has compassion on *you*. In other words, he cares about your feelings. He cares when you're happy. He cares when you're stressed. He cares when you're lonely or overwhelmed or insecure.

Did you know God counts your tears and holds them in his hands?

> You keep track of all my sorrows.
>   You have collected all my tears in your bottle.
>   You have recorded each one in your book.
>
> PSALM 56:8, NLT

But he doesn't stop there. God doesn't just care about your feelings and tears; he invites you to talk to him about them—and I mean *all* your feelings, even the not-so-righteous ones. Even the embarrassing ones. The book of Psalms is filled with examples of emotional people talking to God about their true feelings—raw feelings, desperate feelings, sometimes even sinful feelings—in prayer.

You and I can do the same. That problem you're having with friends? That issue with your mom? That secret temptation you don't know how to talk about? God invites you to talk to him about all of it. He loves the real you—the you with no makeup, no filters, and no retakes. He longs to hear from you—and help you—wherever you are.

THE ROAD AHEAD

In this book we're going to take a close look at what the Bible has to say about feelings. First, we'll examine what God has to say about emotions in general. God himself gave us our emotions, so naturally, he knows how to help us experience them in healthy ways. Can we trust our feelings? Are some feelings good and some not-so-good? Should we encourage ourselves to feel some emotions, and should we limit or avoid others? And how in the world do we learn how to do that?

From there we'll take a closer look at some of the specific difficult feelings that can plague us: insecurity, loneliness, anxiety, sadness, anger, envy, stress. God has things to say about each of those emotions, and I have some practical, Bible-based tips you can apply on your own when you're feeling that way.

As you read, you'll realize that your emotions may be unruly and annoying at times, but they aren't your enemy. In fact, with time and attention, your emotions can become strengths! They can become one of the most sparkling, unique parts of who you are and how you honor God. God has made every one of us with the capacity for big feelings, and he has plans for how he wants to use our feelings for his glory:

- Our compassion can help us comfort hurting friends.

- Our sorrow can help us heal when we've been hurt.
- Our stress (believe it or not!) can help us get things done.
- Our joy can light others' lives.

And on and on go the possibilities.

I started the journey of working on my feelings in middle school and high school, and the truth is, I'm *still* working on my feelings! Emotional growth isn't something we move beyond. You're going to have feelings (including some big ones) for the rest of your life. The sooner you start learning how to manage them, the more balanced and, yes, happy your life is going to be.

I'm not promising that reading this book will make you feel like you're cartwheeling through fields of flowers all day every day for the rest of your life, but I do promise that you can grow. You can learn to handle stress better. You can work through anxious thoughts and sad times with the help of God and his Word. You can make wise decisions using your heart *and* your head—and your Bible. You can better handle the temptation to be insecure or self-consumed or jealous or fill-in-the-blank with the emotion that tempts you most. You can find more happy and become more holy. You can feel closer to God.

Like me, maybe you feel excited about the journey to come. Nervous about the need to grow. Hopeful about making changes. Eager, insecure, understood, comforted, intimidated, encouraged . . . well, you know . . . all the feels.

FEELING YOUR WAY FORWARD

At the end of every chapter, you'll find ideas for applying what you've learned.

The **journal prompts** are questions that will help you think about how the things you learn in this book might apply to your daily life. I am a huge fan of writing down your answers. I've found that the act of moving a pen across paper cements truth more deeply into our hearts and memories—plus, it gives us a record of our thoughts and growth so we can look back and see how God has worked over time.

The **prayer prompts** are passages from the Bible, particularly the Psalms, that communicate various emotions. You can borrow the psalmists' exact words to pray, or you can use them to help inspire your own prayers.

Last, you will find a list of Scriptures about specific feelings—a different feeling for each chapter. These are some of my **lifeline** Scriptures—verses I cling to when all the feels start firing inside and I need the Bible to ground me. I hope these verses will become lifelines for you too.

Journal Prompts

1. Which emotions do you enjoy feeling the most? Which do you find the most difficult or painful?
2. How do you feel about talking to God honestly about your emotions and struggles?
3. How would you describe your overall emotional state in the past month?
4. What emotion would you most like to grow in?
5. If you could change one thing about the way you feel right now, what would it be? Why?

Prayer Prompt

Search me, God, and know my heart;
　　test me and know my anxious thoughts.
See if there is any offensive way in me,
　　and lead me in the way everlasting.

PSALM 139:23-24

Lifelines

Five Scriptures to read when you're anxious:

1. Psalm 131
2. Psalm 37:3-6
3. Psalm 25:4-6
4. Matthew 10:28-31
5. 1 Peter 5:7

CHAPTER 2

FINDING YOUR FEELING TYPE

I'm hiding in my room. Music playing, lights down low, sunset torching the treetops outside my bedroom with golden fire. I'm lying still on my bed, but my thoughts are hardly still. They're swirling, looping, and making me miserable.

"How are you?" Mom asked me half an hour ago, with that worried crease between her eyes.

I shrugged. "Fine."

Mom raised one eyebrow and made her skeptical face, her *I totally don't believe you* face.

I forced a smile that I knew probably made me look consti-pated. "I'm fine. I just need some time alone."

So now here I am, lying on my bed, fine and not fine all at the same time. I'm upset, and I don't even know why. I search my memories:

I said the wrong thing to Sadie today. I'm pretty sure I hurt her feelings. She's totally annoyed. She'll act all weird tomorrow, and we have every class together, so the whole day will be messed up. She won't ask me for the daily Jack update. . . .

The very thought of Jack makes my stomach twist and my cheeks feel hot. I picture his crooked smile, his eyes bright blue— I haven't seen them in person since we moved, but I look at his picture more times a day than I'd like to admit.

Speaking of Jack . . . why hasn't he called? He always calls on Thursdays, but he didn't last night. He's seemed so distracted the last few times we've talked. Is he starting to forget me? Are we over?

My stomach gives a painful lurch. *He's probably forgetting me. I'm totally forgettable. I'm not very funny, I'm not especially pretty, I only listen to dorky '80s music, I read way too much, and I'm kind of a nerd.*

I smack my hands over my face and groan. *Geez, I'm so selfish. All I'm doing is lying here thinking about myself and my problems. God wouldn't want me to do this. He would want me to . . . well, I'm not sure what he'd want me to do. Read my Bible, maybe? Go save the world or something?* A guilty feeling worms its way into my stomach, making me feel a little sick.

My mother's muffled voice drifts up the stairs and into my room: *Mwa-mwa-mwa-mwa-TABLE-mwa-mwa?*

I grimace. She probably needs help setting the table.

A little voice I'm pretty sure is my conscience pipes up: *Maybe God wants you to go help your mom. You could go set the table . . .*

I grimace even more.

I'm not even sure that's what she said. If I go out of my room, I'll have to talk to people.

My conscience gives me a kick in the gut, but I shove it away.

Nah. I'm gonna pretend I didn't hear her. I'd rather lie here alone thinking. Thinking and feeling. Feeling sad, feeling lonely, feeling dumb . . .

* * *

Ever had a day like this? Or a season like this? Everything is wrong and nothing is wrong, all at the same time. Life isn't terrible or anything, but you just Can't. Stop. Feeling.

You're happy-sad-lonely-insecure-annoyed-bored-antsy-giddy-unmotivated-excited, all at the same time. You want . . . *something* . . . but you couldn't even say what it is you want.

You long to be close to God—somehow you know he's the answer to all these feelings swirling inside—and some days you feel connected to him, but other times he feels so far away. So theoretical. God feels very Sunday morning . . . but your real life is lived Monday through Friday, and there's never enough Saturday thrown in.

EMOTIONAL OVERLOAD

For my thirteenth birthday, I got my ears double-pierced. It was kind of the Big Thing to Do in my town at the time, and I felt fabulously sophisticated. But new holes in my ears weren't the only new thing that came with the territory of being thirteen. Before I could say "hormones," I'd started dealing with more feelings than I knew how to name, much less deal with.

Not all of those emotions were bad. Some days I was so excited I didn't understand why I didn't float off the planet and drift into space. I could hardly contain the joy and hope and life-is-gonna-be-amazing I felt inside. Other days I was insecure and lonely—*I'm the only person who's ever thought this, felt this. No one understands. No one cares.* Some days a black cloud followed me around, Eeyore-style. Everyone else was living in sunshine, but I couldn't escape the shadows. I was sad and anxious and felt like crying, and I had no idea why.

Welcome to life with all the feels all the time.

Over time, as I grew in Christ (and in life), I began to realize that I didn't have to be pushed around by my feelings; I actually had the ability to take charge of them. With God's help, we can develop our emotional strength and discover all kinds of beauty and joy in the way he designed us.

It might surprise you to hear this, but your feelings are a gift from God. A gift, not a curse! He himself designed your personality and feelings style. When you were still growing inside your mother's body, God intentionally, painstakingly, and with so much joy it probably made the angels sing, created you just the way he wanted you to be.

The Bible puts it this way:

You created my inmost being;
　　you knit me together in my mother's womb.
I praise you because I am fearfully and wonderfully
　　　made;
　　your works are wonderful,
　　I know that full well.
My frame was not hidden from you
　　when I was made in the secret place,
　　when I was woven together in the depths of the earth.
Your eyes saw my unformed body;
　　all the days ordained for me were written in your book
　　before one of them came to be.

PSALM 139:13-16

And did you know that God himself is deeply emotional? Feelings are not a bad thing—in fact, when we feel deeply, we echo the heartbeat of our Father in heaven! Take a look at this passage from Scripture and all the feelings God demonstrates:

I will tell of the LORD's unfailing love.
　　I will praise the LORD for all he has done.

I will rejoice in his great goodness to Israel,
 which he has granted according to his mercy and love.
He said, "They are my very own people.
 Surely they will not betray me again."
And he became their Savior.
In all their suffering he also suffered,
 and he personally rescued them.
In his love and mercy he redeemed them.
 He lifted them up and carried them
 through all the years.
But they rebelled against him
 and grieved his Holy Spirit.

ISAIAH 63:7-10, NLT

In these few lines, we see God feeling all the feels, just like we do. He feels compassion for his people—intense affection and loyalty. When his people suffer, he hurts along with them; he loves them so much he comes to rescue them at great personal cost. He picks them up and carries them close, like a father carrying his daughter in his arms. *They are my very own people,* he thinks. *They have no reason to betray me.* But then they do reject and betray him, and he feels hurt, disappointed, and sad.

- If you've ever loved someone who let you down, God understands.
- If you've ever loved someone who didn't love you back, God understands.
- If you've ever felt rejected and alone, God understands.
- If you've ever given your whole heart till you could hardly contain all the love swelling inside, God understands.
- If you've ever cared so much that you sacrificed so someone else could be happy, God understands.

When you feel all those big feelings, the positive and the negative, the fun and not-so-fun, you're not just being, you know, a teenager—you're being the emotional person God made you to be. You are being like God. *Feeling* like God.

WHAT KIND OF FEELER ARE YOU?

God made us each different, and there are different types of feelers in the world. Maybe, like me, you're a big feeler. You feel all the feelings, all the day long.

You don't just feel happy—you feel happy with a parade and ice cream and fireworks inside. You don't just feel sad—the world is ending and there's no hope and how can you even get out of bed and do school tomorrow? You don't just feel insecure— you're the only person in the whole world who has ever felt the way you do, and if anyone knew what you were really thinking, they'd banish you from Planet Earth and send you to live alone on Mars.

As a big feeler, you need help figuring out what to do with these gorilla-sized emotions so they don't go stomping all over your life, wrecking your peace, crushing your relationships, and destroying everything in sight. You need to figure out how to handle it when your feelings go roller coaster on you. How to respond when you feel overwhelmed. How to live your life without being bossed around by your feelings. Even if you aren't a big feeler, maybe someone close to you is—a parent, a sibling, a close friend—and the intensity of their emotions sometimes leaks into your life and complicates it. Makes it messy. Confuses you. Even hurts you. You need to know what to do when other people's big feelings affect your life.

Or maybe you're more of a steady feeler. Most days life is good, you feel fine, and you can work through your problems with your head on straight. But sometimes life gets crazy, friends act crazy, and crazy-big feelings come banging on the door of your heart. You need help knowing what to do with big feelings when they come and how to bring your emotions to God.

Maybe you're a reluctant feeler. You prefer thinking to feeling, thank you very much. Logic is way better than emotion. You want life to make sense and be fair and orderly. Maybe feelings confuse you, so you try to ignore them—sometimes you even pretend you don't have them. Maybe you need help figuring out what you feel and how to put it into words. You want to learn more about emotions—don't worry; we're talking fist bumps, not hugs—and figure out what your faith has to do with your feelings.

Each type of feeler is made by God, loved by God, and *liked* by God. Each of the different feeling types needs the others— just imagine how dramatic the world would be if we were *all* big feelers! Big feelers need the steady and reluctant feelers to provide balance and perspective. Likewise, the steady and reluctant feelers need the big feelers to help them feel more, risk more, give more. God designed you the way you are, and he likes you that way. He made you that way because he has plans for your personality, your gifts, and your life.

Me? I'm a **Big Feeler**, with a capital B, a capital F, and extra-bold font. If feelings were animals, mine would be a ginormous gorilla, climbing buildings and taking over the city, not to mention my life. And if you've ever seen one of the old King Kong movies, you know that King Kong wasn't bad—he was just *big*. Big and misunderstood. And when he was misunderstood—well, things got messy.

It took me half a million years to figure out where all my deep feelings fit into my walk with Christ. To realize that our faith is exactly the place—the best place!—to process all our feelings.

Quiz: What Kind of Feeler Are You?

Let's get started by taking a little self-test to figure out your "feelings type." Take a look at these ten statements and mark how often you feel that way: almost always, sometimes, or rarely. Give yourself three points for every "Almost always," two points for every "Sometimes," and one point for "Rarely." Then take a look at the key at the bottom to find your feelings style!

	WHAT KIND OF FEELER ARE YOU?	Almost always	Sometimes	Rarely
1.	I have difficulty separating facts from feelings.			
2.	I am easily overwhelmed.			
3.	People tell me I am too sensitive.			
4.	I experience mood swings.			
5.	I am profoundly moved by beauty or art.			
6.	I feel others' pain as if it were my own.			
7.	I easily put myself in other people's shoes.			
8.	I struggle to shake a mood when it hits.			
9.	Gut feelings and instinct play a role in my decision-making.			
10.	I find it easy to connect with God in worship and prayer.			
	SUBTOTAL			
	TOTAL			

KEY
Almost always = 3
Sometimes = 2
Rarely = 1

RESULTS
23+ = big feeler
15–22 = steady feeler
10–14 = reluctant feeler

So what kind of feeler are you? A big feeler, a steady feeler, or a reluctant feeler? Is your feelings style super obvious, or are you on the border between types? If you're on the border, it may be because you are still figuring yourself out and developing your style—and that's totally fine! You don't have to have yourself all figured out right now—you'll get to know yourself better over time, with a lot of "ooh-I-finally-understand-why-I-do-that" moments along the way.

SUPERSIZE ME!

There's one thing to keep in mind as you figure out your feelings style. Even if you're naturally more of a steady feeler or a reluctant feeler, you are probably going to have a lot of big feelings during your teen years. In other words, you'll probably experience some moments as a part-time big feeler, even if your "full-time" feelings style is more steady or reluctant. Even if you spend most days avoiding strong emotions or just humming steadily along, you'll still have moments when big feelings fly, thanks to these lovely things called hormones.

Can we pause for a second to talk about hormones? I like to think of hormones as having the "Supersize Me" effect. When I was in high school, McDonald's had four sizes of French fries: small, medium, large, and Supersize. Every time you went through the drive-thru and ordered fries, they would ask, "Do you want to Supersize that?" My answer was always a loud *yes*, because who doesn't want more fries? You can never have too many fries!

Teenage hormones work kind of the same way, except they don't give you much choice. Every time you have a feeling, whether it's positive or negative, your hormones are like, *Let's Supersize that feeling!* Because just a little joy won't do—let's break into full-on song and dance! And just a little worry won't do—utter panic and freak-out is way more exciting! And while we're at it, make that a double serving of anger and insecurity!

But as you work your way through this book, you'll find that you actually *can* say no to Supersizing your emotions. It's not always easy, but with the Bible and some basic strategies, you can keep your emotional "orders" down to a reasonable size, one that won't give you a stomachache. (But I still say you should order as many french fries as you want from McDonald's!)

FINDING YOUR GIFTS

Whichever type you are, God made you that way, and you have emotional strengths and gifts to offer the people in your life. Let's take a look at the emotional gifts of each feeling type.

What Reluctant Feelers Have to Offer

- Reluctant feelers help people through hard times. You may be the person your friends turn to when they're upset, because they know you'll stay calm and rational.
- Reluctant feelers focus on what's right. You rarely get caught up in gossip, arguments, and drama, and you aren't afraid to speak up for what's right.
- Reluctant feelers are problem solvers. You are great in a crisis because you can see past the feelings and drama that may distract bigger feelers.
- Reluctant feelers help more emotional people get along. Chances are, you are a peacemaker, a guide, and a leader.

What Steady Feelers Have to Offer

- Steady feelers help other people manage their feelings. You are sympathetic and strong at the same time. This allows you to comfort friends who are experiencing intense emotions without getting overwhelmed yourself.
- Steady feelers can fill a lot of roles. Most likely you are a sympathetic listener and a good problem solver.
- Steady feelers meet people's needs with compassion. Because you know what it's like to feel anxious or insecure or discouraged yourself, you are able to make hurting

people feel understood while still making decisions and helping out.

- Steady feelers motivate and inspire. You are great at connecting on a heart level even as you think, plan, and act.

What Big Feelers Have to Offer

- Big feelers help people understand one another. You serve as a bridge between people. You are great at explaining, "This is what So-and-So is feeling, and this is why."
- Big feelers help people celebrate. You know how to make memories out of moments and savor the good things, which makes you an expert in joy.
- Big feelers feel—and demonstrate—love. When you love, you go all in. And I'm talking about all types of loves, not just romantic love. By showing love—big, brave love—you reflect God's heart.
- Big feelers model vulnerability. You have the capacity for putting feelings into words. You share the deep parts of your soul and help others to do the same.

In the pages to come, I pray you will become more confident in the person God designed you to be—and draw closer to your Designer. I hope you will be giddy-excited about all the great plans God has for you and all the ways he wants to use you and your one-of-a-kind personality and heart.

FANNING YOUR GIFTS INTO FLAME

The apostle Peter encouraged us to use our gifts for God and his people:

Each of you should use whatever gift you have received to serve others, as faithful stewards of God's grace in its various forms. If anyone speaks, they should do so as one who speaks the very words of God. If anyone serves, they should do so with the strength God provides, so that in all things God may be praised through Jesus Christ. To him be the glory and the power for ever and ever. Amen.

1 PETER 4:10-11

Your feelings and design are God's grace to you—and through you, they are God's grace to other people. God wants you to fan your gifts, including your emotional strengths, into flame (see 2 Timothy 1:6)—to use them to honor him and serve people. If you have a heart filled with compassion, share it with the big-heartedness God has given you. If your insights help you notice other people's needs, offer your insights with confidence. If your sense of justice inspires you to serve, meet others' needs with God's strength!

Are you ready to give? Ready to shine? We can all develop and use our strengths to serve God. Let's find out how!

FEELING YOUR WAY FORWARD

Journal Prompts

1. Do you like being the kind of feeler God made you to be? Why or why not?
2. What are your strengths when it comes to emotions? How might you share them more often at home? With friends?
3. Describe a time when you used your gifts to help someone else. How did you feel?

Prayer Prompt

You knit me together in my mother's womb.
I praise you because I am fearfully and wonderfully made;
　your works are wonderful,
　I know that full well.

PSALM 139:13-14

Lifelines

Five Scriptures to read when you're insecure:

1. Psalm 71:5
2. Psalm 139:13-16
3. Ephesians 1:3-6
4. Romans 8:14-17
5. 1 Peter 2:9

CHAPTER 3

WHEN FEELINGS TELL LIES

I pull my oboe apart slowly, nestling each part gently into its blue velvet "bed" inside my case. (If you've never heard of an oboe, it's an instrument that sounds gorgeous when it's played well, but when it's played poorly, it sounds like a dying duck. At this point in my oboe playing, my music no longer sounds like a duck on its deathbed, but the poor thing still sounds mildly nauseated.) I sneak my eyes sideways at the first-chair oboe player, Lily, who is packing up beside me. *This is your chance. Hurry up before she goes to her next class.*

I snap my case shut and shuffle my music around. I'm stalling now. *Maybe I'll wait till tomorrow.*

Mom's voice chirps in my head: *Elizabeth, you'll never make friends at your new school if you don't put yourself out there. Just invite someone over.*

Or I could *not.* I shut my eyes for a second, feeling almost sick with anxiety.

But something brave rises up inside me, and before I realize what I'm doing, I start talking. The words tumble out all mashed together in one enormous word: "HeyLilyyouwannacomeover andhangoutsometime?"

Lily looks up at me, squinting. "Huh? Were you talking to me?"

The brave part of me shrinks back a little, embarrassed. But then it prods me again. I take a breath and make myself slow down. "I was wondering if you wanted to come over and hang out sometime." I force a nervous smile.

"Sure! I'd love to."

"Really?" Something warm and sparkly buzzes inside. "Thanks. I mean, great. I mean . . . yeah."

Lily comes over a few days later, and we hang out and talk for a couple of hours. It's kind of fun, kind of awkward. We talk, look at stuff in my room, wander around outside, then stand around, not sure what else to do.

The next week, Lily invites me over to her house. Again, it's kind of fun but kind of awkward. And the whole time, this little voice in the back of my head keeps saying, *She only invited you over to be polite. You invited her, so now she's inviting you, but she doesn't really want to be your friend.*

I wish I could tell you that I eventually overcame my insecurity, that Lily and I ended up becoming BFFs, but we didn't. We never hung out again. In fact, we hardly talked again, even though we sat next to each other in band every day.

I was just too nervous to ask her over again. Too insecure. Too sure that I wasn't as cool as she was, wasn't as pretty as she was, wasn't as Bostonian as she was. I was different: I said "y'all," I couldn't ice-skate, and I was always worried about what people thought of me. Why would someone like Lily want to be friends with someone like me?

*   *   *

This was one of many times when one of my emotions took over—in this case, insecurity. Insecurity, with its booming voice and strong opinions, fed me a bunch of lies:

> *You're not cool.*
> *Other people have interesting things to say, but you don't.*
> *You're different. Weird.*
> *Lily isn't interested in being your friend.*
> *And it's not just Lily . . . no one wants to be friends with you.*

I believed my insecure feelings, and they robbed me of a potential friendship.

This brings up one of the most confusing truths about our feelings: our feelings don't always tell us the truth.

But wait. Can that be right? Our feelings *feel* so real. They come from deep inside us, and they're basically a part of us, so they have to be true, right?

BUT IT FEELS SO REAL . . .

Let's look at an example in the Bible of someone who listened to their feelings when their feelings weren't telling them the truth. Saul was a young rabbi, or teacher, who had trained under the best teachers in Israel. He was fiercely devoted to God, and he followed God's ways as perfectly as he could.

Saul devoted his life to honoring the name of God and making sure the Jewish people did the same. So when he heard about a group of Jews who were going around telling everyone that their teacher, Jesus, was the Son of God and that Jesus had risen from the dead and gone into heaven—well, Saul was appalled. Claiming to be God was a terrible sin!

Saul was passionate, determined to defend the name of God

and the purity of the Jewish faith. He set out to stop the lies. He was so determined to defeat these lying "Christians" that he even took part in killing one of them: a man named Stephen. And killing one Christian wasn't enough—Saul wanted to stop them all, in every city:

> Saul was uttering threats with every breath and was eager to kill the Lord's followers. So he went to the high priest. He requested letters addressed to the synagogues in Damascus, asking for their cooperation in the arrest of any followers of the Way he found there. He wanted to bring them—both men and women—back to Jerusalem in chains.
>
> ACTS 9:1-2, NLT

But as Saul was on his way to Damascus to arrest Christians, something surprising happened. This is the way I picture it:

> "Hurry!" Saul shouts to his companions. "I want to get there by nightfall." With every step, his determination grows fiercer. *I must stop these blasphemers. They corrupt our religion and dishonor God. How could they call this man Jesus, this fraud, the Son of God?*
>
> Fury rises in him, a hungry flame. He feeds the fire and stokes it hotter. *This must be what it feels like to be filled with God's holy fire,* he thinks. *I must see this through. I must stop these Christians, kill them for dishonoring God. I've never felt anything so strongly in my life.*
>
> But then a light flashes—bright, hot, blinding. Saul stumbles to his knees with a cry, an arm up to shield his eyes. A voice, deep as thunder, booms: "Saul, Saul!"
>
> Saul feels the rumble of the voice deep inside his body, as if the earth were shaking.

"Why do you persecute me?"

"Wh-who are you, Lord?" Saul stammers, his voice weak as a kitten's mewl.

"I am Jesus, whom you are persecuting."

The words strike like a spear to Saul's gut. His breath stops, the world spins, his thoughts fly. *No. It can't be. And yet—*

The voice thunders again. It surrounds him, rings inside him, sets his very bones to trembling. "Get up, go into the city, and you will be told what to do."

The light disappears, and as it fades, the world goes dim—gray, fuzzy, then completely dark. Saul rubs his eyes—still nothing. He cries out in fear. He hears voices—familiar voices, the voices of his friends—surrounding him, but he can see nothing.

"What was that? Brother Saul, are you all right? What happened?"

Saul buries his head in his knees. When he speaks, tears choke the words. "My brothers, we have been wrong. So very wrong." He sucks in a shaky breath. "Take my hand and lead me into Damascus." (Based on Acts 9:1-8.)

* * *

What a shocking day this must have been for Saul. A before-and-after day. A stopped-in-his-tracks (literally) day. A day when he found out that everything he'd felt and believed with all his heart had been wrong.

Saul ended up spending three days fasting and praying, coming to terms with his mistake. Then he was baptized as a follower of Jesus. He stopped persecuting Christians and began preaching Christ! He later changed his name from Saul to Paul—you probably know him as the apostle Paul, the man who ended up writing almost half of the books of the New Testament.

Paul's conversion story shows us one of the big problems with our feelings: as convincing as they are, as much as we instinctively trust them, we can't trust *all* our feelings. Our feelings aren't always reliable. For example:

- Some feelings make us feel bad when we should feel good; other feelings make us feel good when we should feel bad.
- Some feelings misinterpret the facts.
- Some feelings twist the truth.
- Some feelings only tell part of the story.
- Some feelings exaggerate.
- Some feelings tell outright lies.

Ugh. Those truths are kind of discouraging, aren't they? It's kind of like when you find out the good guy in a movie isn't good at all. Or when you find out a friend you trusted isn't your friend after all.

Saul *felt like* he was doing the right thing, but his feelings were wrong. Saul *felt like* he knew what to do about Jesus and his followers, but his feelings led him astray. His feelings even caused him to commit murder! Saul's feelings weren't telling him the truth. It turned out his feelings were just feelings, not facts.

Now let's think about times when our own feelings don't tell us the truth. Have you ever experienced any of these situations?

- You feel like your friend is mad at you, but she isn't mad at you at all.
- You feel like you failed a test, but you actually got a good grade.
- You feel like you're bad at a certain skill, but once you get more practice, it turns out you're pretty good at it.

Feelings Workshop

Let's workshop some feelings! Fill out this chart with some feelings you experience today. The first row is filled in for you as an example.

A FEELING I HAD TODAY	WHAT PROMPTED THAT FEELING?	WAS THAT FEELING TRUE—OR JUST A FEELING?	WHAT IS THE TRUTH?	WHAT SCRIPTURE COULD HELP ME WITH THIS FEELING?
I'm the only one who was lost in math class today. I must be dumb.	No one else looked confused. No one asked any questions.	Feeling. It's unlikely that everyone else in class understood the lesson. I bet someone else was confused too.	Sometimes people don't ask questions even though they're confused. I'm not dumb—I'm just having a hard time understanding a particular concept.	I am fearfully and wonderfully made (Psalm 139:14).

- You feel like life is terrible and won't ever get any better, but once you get a good night's sleep (and maybe something to eat!), you see that life isn't that bad after all.

Our feelings don't always tell us the truth. Our feelings are not facts!

Now, how does it change your life when you understand that feelings aren't facts? It means you don't have to be trapped by your feelings. It means you have power over your feelings. It puts *you* in the driver's seat of your heart—you are in charge; you are steering the car—instead of your emotions.

It gives you permission to step back from all you feel to ask yourself a simple question: I *feel* a certain way . . . but is this feeling *true*?

FEELINGS VERSUS FACTS

So how can we tell the difference between feelings and facts? I like to break this process down into three simple steps:

1. Acknowledge
2. Assess
3. Address or adiós!

Step 1: Acknowledge your feelings.

To *acknowledge* your feelings means that you take the time to identify them. I like to write my feelings down on paper, because feelings are slippery shape-changers, and they can be hard to identify when they're just floating around in a messy tangle inside your head and heart.

So let's revisit my insecure feelings toward my would-be friend Lily. If I'd followed these steps back then, I would have acknowledged my feelings by writing them down like this:

I feel insecure with Lily.
I feel like she's cooler than I am.
I feel like she probably doesn't want to be friends.

Step 2: Assess your feelings.

When you *assess* your feelings, you take an honest, hard look at them. You don't automatically assume that your feelings are right; you ask your feelings some questions. In order to assess my feelings about Lily, I would have had a mental conversation with myself, something like this:

Why do you feel insecure with Lily?
Uh, because she's cooler than I am.
Why do you think she's cooler than you are?
Well, she's pretty.
And?
She's one chair better than me in band.
And?
I don't really know why else. I just feel like she's cooler than I am
and probably doesn't want to be my friend.
Let's talk about that one a little more. What proof do you have
that Lily doesn't want to be your friend?
I guess I don't have any proof. But I really feel that way.
She came over to your house when you asked her, and then she
invited you over, right?
Yes.
Usually people don't hang out with people they don't want to be
friends with, right?
Uh . . . yeah. I guess that's right.
So actually, the evidence suggests that Lily does want to be your
friend, doesn't it? You have zero evidence that she doesn't

want to be your friend, and two examples where she has shown interest in being your friend.

Wow, okay. Yeah. I guess that's right. Maybe she does actually want to be my friend.

Do you see how this little internal dialogue forces me to stop sitting around feeling paralyzed by insecurity? It forces me to label my feelings, and it forces my feelings to prove they are true!

Step 3: Address or adiós your feelings!

ADDRESS YOUR FEELINGS.

When we *address* our feelings, we tackle them head on. We don't just sit around stressing and complaining and angsting over insecurity or worry or fear—we face it. We do something about the feeling. And yes, doing something takes courage!

So let's return to the Lily example.

Once I've assessed my feelings, I have a decision to make. If it turns out my feelings are correct, then perhaps I need to do something about them.

Let's say my internal dialogue revealed a problem in my relationship with Lily. What if I remembered that I'd hurt her feelings in band one day and *that* was the source of the awkwardness and insecurity between us? In that case, I might need to address the issue.

How might I do that? Well, I could talk to Lily. I could say, "Hey, remember that day when I hurt your feelings? I'm sorry for what I said. I wasn't thinking, and I'm sorry I made you feel bad."

And then I would have an opportunity to work things out with her. Maybe she would offer forgiveness and we'd start over. Maybe the reason for my insecurity would be resolved.

This strategy can work in other areas of your life too. Let's say you're feeling worried about your grade in a class. You feel sure you're going to fail. Your assessment of your feelings goes something like this:

Why am I worried about my grade?
Because I have three zeroes for not turning in my homework,
  and I did badly on the last test because I waited till the
  night before to cram.

Aha! It turns out your feelings have a cause—something you can address—and change!

So what can you do? First, you can make some changes to your study habits: you can keep up with your homework and start studying for your next test earlier. Second, you might also go to your teacher and ask for some makeup work or extra credit. (It never hurts to ask!)

Guess what happens when you address your feeling by making changes—even simple ones? You take back control of your feelings. Your feelings aren't in control anymore—*you* are. Just like that, you've turned the tables on your worry. You've stopped sitting around feeling worried and helpless, and you have *done something* about what's bothering you. You still feel concerned about your grade, but you no longer feel powerless and overwhelmed—and that makes all the difference.

ADIÓS YOUR FEELINGS.
But what if you assess a feeling and realize that it simply isn't true? Going back to the Lily example, my assessment revealed that my insecurity was a feeling without any evidence to back it up. *I was feeling insecure for no reason.*

So that means it's time to say "adiós" (and we say goodbye in Spanish because we're fancy like that)—to that insecurity. *Get out of my head, insecurity! I'm not listening to your lies anymore. I'm listening to facts and God's Word instead.* It's time to give that feeling over to God in prayer, asking him to help you to think and feel differently. It's time to let it go and set your thoughts on other things.

Myths about Feelings

These statements are common misconceptions about feelings. Find a Scripture or fact to prove why each statement is not true (or not *always* true).

MYTH	SCRIPTURE OR FACT THAT PROVES IT'S NOT TRUE
If I feel something, it must be true.	
I can only obey God when I feel like obeying him.	
If I'm a Christian, then I will always feel like doing the right thing.	
The main way God speaks to us is through our feelings.	
I'm going to feel this way forever.	
Feelings should lead the way in my decision-making.	
I can't help the way I feel.	
I can't change the way I feel.	

AFTERBURN

Here's something to keep in mind: after you address or adiós a feeling, it may not go away immediately. Our emotions don't switch on and off like light bulbs—*I'm feeling down, so I'll spend a few minutes praying, and the moment I say amen I'll feel happy!* Feelings are more like fireworks. You know how when you watch fireworks, you can still see the outline of the lights on the back of your eyelids for a while? Like your eyes still think there's a party even though the fireworks are over? When you know the lights are just afterburn, it's easier to ignore them until they disappear. I've found that, just as fireworks leave a lingering neon glow on our eyes, so strong feelings can leave a residual outline on our hearts—a sense-memory that fades over time.

Even after you tell a false feeling goodbye, you may still feel a little funky for a while, but less funky than before, and eventually not funky at all. For steady and reluctant feelers, the afterburn may be subtle—just a vague sense of feeling down or unsettled or "off." For big feelers, the afterburn may shine pretty bright for a while—the lingering feeling may still *feel* strong and convincing even after you've said adiós. Sometimes it might stick around long enough to make you doubt yourself: *Did I actually deal with this emotion? Was my assessment wrong? Should I have listened to that feeling after all?*

When afterburn strikes, I like to keep in mind what my dad calls the Twenty-Minute Rule. Our brains and our stomachs operate on a twenty-minute communication delay, meaning that when you eat, it takes your brain about twenty minutes to get your stomach's message saying, *Hey, you with the food! I'm full! Stop eating!* (And this explains the sudden I-feel-like-I-just-ate-a-whole-watermelon stomachache you get whenever you inhale your food too fast!)

The principle in Dad's Twenty-Minute Rule applies to our emotions, too: after you address or adiós a feeling, don't expect immediate relief; give your emotions at least twenty minutes to catch up to your prayers and decisions. I know it sounds simplistic, and it may not always apply when gorilla-sized feelings come calling, but it really does help. The Twenty-Minute Rule helps me stick to my decisions and not get discouraged when emotional relief comes more slowly than I think it should.

In time, with practice and prayer, we can learn to take charge of our feelings instead of letting them push us around. When you assess a feeling and realize it isn't true, I give you permission, by the authority vested in me by Walt Disney and by our mutual big feelings, to pull an Elsa and *let it go*!

FEELING YOUR WAY FORWARD

Journal Prompts

1. Everyone struggles with different feelings. Some people wrestle often with insecurity; others face constant anxiety. Which feelings make it most difficult for you to think clearly and find the facts?
2. Describe a time when you acted on a feeling that turned out to be false. What can help you to see through false feelings in the future?
3. Try the exercise on page 38. Acknowledge a specific feeling you've been struggling with, then assess it using Scripture and facts as a guide. If it turns out to be a valid feeling, address it the best you can. If your assessment reveals that the feeling is untrue, tell it "Adiós!"

Prayer Prompt

How can a young person stay on the path of purity?
    By living according to your word.
I seek you with all my heart;
    do not let me stray from your commands.
I have hidden your word in my heart
    that I might not sin against you.

PSALM 119:9-11

Lifelines

Five Scriptures to help you take charge of your thoughts:

1. Philippians 4:8
2. Romans 13:14
3. Colossians 3:2
4. Psalm 139:23-24
5. 2 Corinthians 10:5

CHAPTER 4

WHO'S CALLING THE SHOTS?

We've heard the message a thousand ways, in songs and stories, books and movies:

> *Listen to your heart.*
> *Follow your gut.*
> *Your heart will never steer you wrong.*
> *You'll know what to do because it will feel right.*
> *The stronger the feeling, the truer it is!*

Even Obi Wan Kenobi got in on the message when he told Luke Skywalker, "Act on instinct. . . . Stretch out with your feelings."

And it all sounds wise; our heads can't help but nod in agreement. After all, Obi Wan would never lead us astray! But there's just one little problem: none of it's true.

I can hear you now: "Wait, whaaaaaaaat? You mean *Star Wars* and the Disney movies have been misleading me all these years?

Next are you going to tell me that emojis aren't a legit form of communication?"

It's upsetting, right? Now, I have nothing against Disney and *Star Wars*. I'm a total fangirl. But hang with me while we talk this out, because this is one of the most important truths we're going to talk about in this book.

We've already established that our feelings aren't always trustworthy. Because of that, we can't live by our feelings. Your feelings should *enrich* your life, but they shouldn't *guide* your life. Our feelings can't be our standard for truth and decision-making.

Let's take food as an example. If I made my food choices based on feelings alone, I'm sorry to tell you that I would live off coffee, dark chocolate with sea salt caramel, and movie popcorn. My mouth would be happy while I was eating, and my brain would send me all kinds of happy hormones triggered by the sugar and caffeine and salt, but after a few "meals" like this, I'd start feeling sick. If I kept up this eat-by-my-feelings diet, before long I would develop all kinds of health problems. My body would be deprived of the nutrients it needs from fruits and vegetables. My muscles would be begging for protein!

In the same way, we can't live by our feelings. Sometimes we crave too much of what we should have only occasionally. Sometimes we avoid things that are good for us. And sometimes we devour things that aren't good for us at all.

So if we can't always trust our feelings or live by our feelings, how do we make decisions? What's our guide, and what's our standard? For Christians, the answer is simple and clear: God is our guide, and his Word is our standard.

GOD AS YOUR GUIDE

True story: I've gotten turned around in my own neighborhood more than once. When I'm driving, and my gut tells me to turn left, I've learned that it's better to turn right instead—then *maybe* I'll end up in the correct place.

As you can imagine, my horrible sense of direction means I'm utterly dependent on my phone's GPS to get me places. But sometimes my phone loses its signal while I'm driving, and the map goes blank. That's when I pretty much start hyperventilating. And other times my maps aren't up to date, and my phone tells me to turn down roads that don't exist. I immediately fly into panic mode. Without an accurate map to guide me, I'm helpless!

In life we need more than maps to guide us—we need spiritual guides to show us the way in our decisions and relationships. And God is the one who can guide our lives. If you really think about it, isn't that a huge relief? Think about how difficult it can be to navigate right from wrong, healthy from unhealthy. Now imagine trying to figure all of that out by yourself, without God to lead you. Life would be a total guessing game! We'd be lost and confused, just like I am when my map app betrays me.

God's "maps" for your life are always up to date. He will never accidentally send you down a nonexistent road or into a dangerous area. And God will never "lose signal." No matter what guidance you need, he's always there to point you in the right direction.

What a comfort it is to let God guide us instead of our feelings. Think about some of the differences between our feelings and God's feelings:

- Our feelings can change day by day, hour by hour (sometimes minute by minute!), but God is always the same: "I am the LORD, and I do not change," he promises us (Malachi 3:6, NLT).
- Our feelings don't always tell us the truth, but God is always truthful (see Hebrews 6:18).

- Our feelings aren't always fair. (Ever gotten angry at someone when it wasn't really their fault? Ahem, siblings? Cough, parents? Teachers?) But God is always fair (see Psalm 103:6).
- Our feelings are sometimes unloving (even toward ourselves). But God is love (see 1 John 4:8; Psalm 103:17).
- Our feelings don't always make sense. But God is all-knowing and all-wise (see Psalm 104:24; Jeremiah 10:12; Isaiah 55:9).
- Our feelings sometimes make snap judgments based on inaccurate or incomplete information. But God knows everything, so his judgments are always correct, always fair, always true (see Psalm 9:8; 96:13).

THE WORD AS YOUR STANDARD

God is not only our guide; he has also given us the Bible as our standard. A standard is what we turn to when we aren't sure what's right. A standard tells us right from wrong and helps us make decisions. As the standard for life, God's Word teaches us how to live, how to please him, and how to be saved.

> Your word, LORD, is eternal;
>   it stands firm in the heavens. . . .
> Your laws endure to this day,
>   for all things serve you.
> If your law had not been my delight,
>   I would have perished in my affliction.
> I will never forget your precepts,
>   for by them you have preserved my life.
>
> PSALM 119:89, 91-93

We can turn to Scripture any time we aren't sure what to do, how to live, or even what to feel. When our feelings get knotted, the Bible can help us untangle them. And it can help us discern the truth when our feelings are untrustworthy.

Here are some of the times we need to believe God instead of our feelings:

- Believe God when he tells you that you are his beloved daughter (see Ephesians 1:3-6).
- Believe God when he tells you that you are forgiven in Christ (see Ephesians 1:7-14).
- Believe God when he tells you that he will strengthen you in temptation (see 1 Corinthians 10:13).
- Believe God when he tells you that he will see you through hard times (see Isaiah 43:1-7).
- Believe God when he tells you that hard times don't mean God is mad at you (see Hebrews 12:4-11).
- Believe God when he tells you that you are still forgiven and saved when you make mistakes (see 1 John 2:1-2).
- Believe God when he tells you that sin will hurt you (see Psalm 32:8-10; Deuteronomy 30:15-18).
- Believe that God's way works even when you don't want to do things his way (see Proverbs 3:5).
- Believe God's Word even when you're in the middle of an emotional storm (see Matthew 7:24-27).

Let's dive a little deeper into that last point. We all have times when our emotions ratchet up to hurricane levels. Like hurricanes, our inner storms feed off of emotional heat. When we keep filling ourselves with fear, worry, anger, guilt, and other negative emotions, the swirl of feelings grows bigger, spins wilder, and blows harder. Emotional storms only peter out when we stop feeding them. The next time an emotional hurricane batters your heart, try clinging to a cooler, more logical source, like the truth of God's

Word, logical thoughts, or sound advice from a godly friend. The winds will slow and the rain will ease. Eventually the clouds will part and the sun will shine again.

WHEN YOU DON'T FEEL LIKE DOING RIGHT

Can we be honest? Sometimes our feelings don't agree with what God says. Sometimes we don't like teachings we find in the Bible. Don't worry—this book isn't going to burst into flames because we admitted those things. It's just *true*: we don't always like God's way, and we don't always want to do the right thing!

Can we be even more honest? Obeying God won't always make you feel happy right away—in fact, it might make your life more difficult and complicated. Doing the right thing is often much harder than sinning. In the long run, God's ways will make you happiest, but sometimes, in the short run, God's ways are difficult. They may require you to act selflessly, make a sacrifice, or take a stand.

For all these reasons, we can't base our walk of faith on how we feel. When we make Jesus the Lord of our lives, that means he's in charge—even when his ways are hard. When we make Jesus the Lord of our lives, that means we follow his ways even when we don't feel like it.

If you think about it, this happens in life a lot. We *all* have to do things we don't feel like doing. Take this lovely (and by "lovely" I mean "disgusting") example from my life:

* * *

I'm fifteen, and I'm babysitting for two boys down the street. It's been a good morning so far: playing with Play-Doh and eating snacks and running around in the backyard. I head into the kitchen to make some lunch, but when I call the boys to come eat, the youngest brother doesn't show.

"Danny?" I start poking around the living room. No Danny. "Hey, buddy, it's not time to play hide-and-seek." I head down the darkened hallway toward the boys' room. And then I hear it: a gurgling sound, followed by the splash of liquid hitting the floor. The stench hits me the moment my foot crosses the threshold, and I gag, instinctively covering my nose with one hand.

Danny is standing in a lake of vomit in the middle of his bedroom. His mouth is dripping chunky goo; his eyes are leaking tears. He looks up at me, chin trembling, and says, "I frew up."

Everything in me wants to close my eyes, plug my nose, and run home. I don't feel like dealing with this. Not even a teeny-tiny bit. I didn't realize I was signing up for barf duty when I agreed to babysit, but here we are. I'm in charge, and little Danny needs me. So I breathe through my mouth and start moving.

I'll spare you the gory cleanup details—except to tell you that before the afternoon was over, I would end up sliding underneath Danny's bed on my stomach, trying hard not to get barf on my clothes—or breathe—as I stretched to reach all the splatter. I hope you never have to experience this kind of a babysitting horror. I still twitch thinking about it.

I didn't feel like cleaning up throw-up. I felt like ignoring the mess and running home. But this was part of my job, so I did it.

There will be many, many, many things in life—and in your faith—that you don't want to do. Your feelings will tell you one thing; the Bible will tell you another. And in those moments, when you're tempted to glance at someone else's paper or pass along a juicy bit of gossip or hide something you know you should tell your parents, the wisest call is to follow the Bible instead of your feelings.

The Bible calls this "denying yourself." It's a basic part of the call to be a follower of Christ.

[Jesus] said to the crowd, "If any of you wants to be my follower, you must *give up your own way*, take up your cross daily, and follow me. If you try to hang on to your life, you will lose it. But if you give up your life for my sake, you will save it. And what do you benefit if you gain the whole world but are yourself lost or destroyed?"

LUKE 9:23-25, NLT (EMPHASIS ADDED)

Following Jesus sometimes means doing things you don't feel like doing. It means giving up your own way of doing things. It means losing your life—your will, your choices, your desires—for the sake of Jesus. And before you start feeling guilty that this is such a struggle, keep in mind that this is hard for *every* Christian in the world. Struggling doesn't mean you're extra sinful!

Take a look at what the apostle Paul wrote about this:

The moment I decide to do good, sin is there to trip me up. I truly delight in God's commands, but it's pretty obvious that not all of me joins in that delight. Parts of me covertly rebel, and just when I least expect it, they take charge.

ROMANS 7:21-23, MSG

You know that picture you sometimes see in cartoons of the little angel on one shoulder and the little devil on the other? That image is more accurate than we like to admit! Part of us loves God and delights in his ways, but another part of us, our sinful nature, doesn't. Our sinful nature desires the opposite of what God desires: "The sinful nature is always hostile to God" (Romans 8:7, NLT). Our feelings are at war within us!

We can't help being tempted; it's part of our human nature. But guess what? There's one thing we want more than anything else, more than any sin or comfort or compromise: we want to please God. We just have to remind ourselves of that when temptation comes calling.

Each of the feeling types may be tempted differently when God's ways don't match their own desires. Big feelers may be tempted to panic or give in to dramatic worst-case scenario thoughts: *If I do this Hard Thing for God, my life might fall apart! My friends might turn on me!* Steady feelers may want to stuff their feelings and ignore their conscience, doing whatever is most comfortable or convenient. Reluctant feelers may be tempted to ignore emotions in their decision-making—to disregard the way sinful choices could affect their relationships with God or others.

Our feelings will jerk us all around, sometimes leading us down unrighteous paths; that's why we turn to God and the Bible for answers and direction. God and the Bible will never lie to us. They won't mislead us or cause us to compromise. They will always tell us what's right and true.

And best of all, when you fight to do the right thing, God is right there with you, standing by your side to strengthen and help you—not just with your actions, but also with your heart.

> Work hard to show the results of your salvation, obeying
> God with deep reverence and fear. *For God is working*
> *in you, giving you the desire and the power to do what*
> *pleases him.*
> PHILIPPIANS 2:12-13, NLT (EMPHASIS ADDED)

How encouraging! God can give you both the desire *and* the power to please him! Whenever you struggle—whenever that desire and power feel far away—turn to God in prayer and ask him to fulfill this promise in your heart.

JESUS' EXAMPLE

Now if you're still feeling guilty about struggling to do the right thing, keep this in mind: even Jesus didn't always feel like doing God's will. Think about when he was in the garden of Gethsemane. In Matthew 26:36-46, we read about the night before he was arrested. He spent all night in prayer, begging God not to send him to the Cross. Did you ever realize that despite his commitment to fulfilling God's call, Jesus didn't *want* to suffer and die?

He dreaded the pain and anguish, and begged God to spare him if there was another way. "I am overwhelmed with sorrow to the point of death," he told his friends. To God he said, "If it is possible, let this cup of suffering be taken away from me. Yet I want your will to be done, not mine" (Matthew 26:39, NLT). Jesus' desire was to live! His desire was not to suffer. But he wanted God's will more than he wanted his own. And that's what Christianity comes down to, isn't it? That's what helps us say no to sin and yes to God. That's what helps us say no to our feelings when they disagree with God: *we want God's will more than we want our own.*

And Jesus had other feelings and desires besides dread. He felt love for God and love for you and me. He felt concern for us, compassion for our sins. He wanted to save us, so he decided to listen to his feelings of love instead of his feelings of fear. Going to the Cross was the hardest thing he'd ever done—the hardest thing anyone has ever done—and yet he did it out of obedience to God and love for you and me.

Jesus' example is a huge encouragement to us whenever we're tempted, battling our own desires versus God's desires.

You can imitate Jesus' example:

- when you want to click on a video you know God wouldn't want you to watch;
- when you want to participate in a gossipy conversation;

- when you want to lie to escape consequences;
- when you want to text that boy who's not the best influence on you;
- when you want to stay lost in your thoughts, locked in your room, instead of reaching out to someone else.

Here's an encouraging Scripture to cling to whenever you face temptation:

> The temptations in your life are no different from what others experience. And God is faithful. He will not allow the temptation to be more than you can stand. When you are tempted, he will show you a way out so that you can endure.
>
> 1 CORINTHIANS 10:13, NLT

As we talked about earlier, following God's ways won't always make you happy. But many, many times *it will.* And it will make you happy in much deeper and longer-lasting ways than anything else will. Even though denying yourself feels difficult in the moment, it feels good later on. When you click away from that website or walk away from that unkind conversation or speak that truth in love, your conscience is clear. A clear conscience is worth far more than any momentary pleasure sin has to offer.

And there's more:

- It feels good to please God.
- It feels good to grow spiritually.
- It feels good to have a victory.
- It feels good to find out you're stronger than you thought.

And feeling good . . . well, it feels good!

FEELING YOUR WAY FORWARD

Journal Prompts

1. When do you find it most difficult to obey God? What helps you get your feelings in line with his will?
2. Describe a time when you didn't want to do things God's way but you followed him anyway. How did things turn out? How did you feel?
3. List three thoughts that heat up your emotions when you're upset. Now list three thoughts that could help your emotions cool down.

Prayer Prompt

Show me your ways, LORD,
    teach me your paths.
Guide me in your truth and teach me,
    for you are God my Savior,
      and my hope is in you all day long.

PSALM 25:4-5

Lifelines

Five Scriptures to help you grow in putting God first:

1. Luke 9:23-26
2. Matthew 6:19-21
3. Matthew 11:28-30
4. Matthew 13:44-46
5. 2 Corinthians 5:14-15

CHAPTER 5

WHAT GOD HAS TO SAY TO YOU

Friday night. Brooklyn, New York. A church youth gathering. Soaring ceilings, bad lighting, not enough mirrors in the bathrooms for all the girls who are elbowing for space in front of them. I give up—*I really hope my mascara isn't running*—and head back into the semidark fellowship hall filled with teenage boys who are all wrestling and shouting for no apparent reason.

The speaker calls us to sit down, and I find a place to sit cross-legged on the concrete floor. She begins: "Have you ever wanted to hear God say, 'I love you'?"

Unconsciously, I lean forward.

She continues. "Well, I have, so I started searching the Bible to see if I could find a place where he actually says those words." She pauses, then grins. "I found one. It's in Isaiah 43, starting in verse 1." She flips open her Bible and starts to read:

"This is what the LORD says—
    he who created you, Jacob,
    he who formed you, Israel:

'Do not fear, for I have redeemed you;
 I have summoned you by name; you are mine.'"

The speaker pauses. "Do you realize God has called each of you *by name*? You are his. You belong to him."

By name.

A little tingle starts in the base of my spine.

His.

The tingle crawls up to my neck, leaving a trail of goose bumps. She starts reading again:

"When you pass through the waters,
 I will be with you;
and when you pass through the rivers,
 they will not sweep over you.
When you walk through the fire,
 you will not be burned;
 the flames will not set you ablaze.
For I am the LORD your God,
 the Holy One of Israel, your Savior . . .

Since you are precious and honored in my sight,
 and *because I love you*,
I will give people in exchange for you,
 nations in exchange for your life." (emphasis added)

"Do you understand what this means?" the speaker asks. "Do you hear—really hear—what God is saying to you? When you walk through fire and water; when you go through hard things; when you walk through the hallways alone at school; when you sit in the dark in your bedroom at night, wondering if you are loved, God is with you. No matter what hard thing is happening in your life, God is with you, and he loves you. You are precious to him."

My heart is humming with joy. I roll the words around inside, letting them fill me up, easing the constant ache of insecurity, the ever-present questions: *Am I good enough? Does God really love me?*

Through fire.
Through water.
Precious.
I love you.

I go home that night and find that verse in my Bible again, underline it, and put a little heart next to it in the margin. I sit thinking about it, letting it warm me from the inside.

* * *

That night was one of the first times I realized that a single passage of Scripture could change my life. After that night, my walk with God was a little different. My view of myself was a little different. My joy, my hope, my confidence—everything began to shift. That passage began a wonderful work in me.

That's the power of the Bible. I've read thousands of books in my life—I could happily spend the rest of my life in a library!— but no book has ever changed me the way the Bible has. It contains the words of God, the voice of God.

And the voice of God is a mighty thing:

The voice of the LORD is powerful;
the voice of the LORD is majestic.
The voice of the LORD breaks the cedars. . . .

The voice of the LORD strikes
with flashes of lightning.
The voice of the LORD shakes the desert;
the LORD shakes the Desert of Kadesh.

The voice of the LORD twists the oaks
    and strips the forests bare.
    And in his temple all cry, "Glory!"

PSALM 29:4-5, 7-9

We can find God's voice—and even better, his heart—in the pages of Scripture. Those words aren't boring or flat—they're a source of strength and comfort meant to be used in our daily life.

LIFELINE VERSES

The Bible is the standard for how we live, but it's so much more than that: it's also our source of hope, joy, and confidence. That night in New York, I found one of my first lifeline verses—a verse I would read countless times throughout high school and college. When loneliness or insecurity caught me in their terrible rip current, I could grab on to Isaiah 43, and it would pull me free. When guilt or shame coiled around my ankles, these verses could cut me loose. Even now, reading Isaiah 43 feels like wrapping myself in a warm blanket on a winter night: it reminds me that I am safe. Loved. Protected.

We all have certain feelings we struggle with over and over again. Maybe you wrestle with worry or insecurity or fear. Or maybe you're plagued by guilt or anxiety or impatience. Whatever your struggle is, I encourage you to find lifeline verses that speak to your specific situation.

Maybe you're thinking, *That sounds great, but when I read the Bible, all the words run together. It's kind of boring. I just don't connect with it.* If so, you are not alone in feeling that way! It can take time to learn how to read the Bible in ways that make it come alive in your heart. Read on to find ways you can learn to love your Bible—and find your lifelines.

GETTING STARTED

When I first started trying to have morning devotion times, I quickly got discouraged. I told my mentor, "I don't understand how you read the Bible and always learn all these interesting things!" Shame crept hot onto my cheeks. "When I read it, either it's boring because I've read it before or it's confusing because I don't understand what I'm supposed to get out of it."

She smiled and pulled me in for a hug. "Don't get discouraged! The more you read the Bible, the better you'll get at it."

And you know what? She was right. I stuck with it, and now I truly love reading my Bible. I'm not saying the words leap off the page and set my heart singing every day or anything, but I'm rarely bored!

Need a few tips to help you get started? There are many different ways to read your Bible. None of them is necessarily "right" or better than the other; they're just different strategies you can experiment with.

First, make sure you're reading a translation you can understand. Some translations use old-fashioned language that sounds beautiful but is formal and tough to understand. Two of my favorite translations are the New International Version and the New Living Translation. If you have a Bible app on your phone, you can try reading different versions. Once you find a version that works for you, it's time to figure out what to read.

If you're not sure where to start, you can:

- Read the Bible one book at a time. (I often recommend that new Bible readers start with the book of Mark. It tells the story of Jesus' life, and it's a fast-paced read.)
- Study a particular person in the Bible. Read everything the Bible has to say about that person and see what lessons (good and bad!) you can learn from their life.

- Choose a topic and search for Scriptures that address it. If you're reading on a Bible app, you can find passages by typing a word or phrase into the search bar. You can also use a concordance—a book that organizes Bible verses by topic. Some topics to try are peace, joy, anxiety, compassion, serving the poor, following Jesus, fear, patience, love, and self-control.
- Choose a character trait of God to study. You might study his kindness, patience, power, anger, or forgiveness. (Again, you can use search tools in a Bible app or a concordance to help you find verses.)
- Choose a spiritual discipline you want to grow in (such as prayer or Bible study or evangelism) and find Scriptures that offer guidance on this topic.

QUESTIONS TO ASK AS YOU READ

When you're reading the Bible, it helps to keep a journal beside you so you can jot down some notes. I always remember what I'm studying better if I take notes. (This also keeps my mind from wandering!)

Even if you've read a passage or story many times, you can still learn new things from it. I'm always amazed at the way the Bible comes alive to me in new ways depending on what I'm going through at the time. Scriptures that didn't touch me deeply last year may be lifesavers this year because my circumstances and struggles have changed.

Here are some questions I find helpful to think about as I'm studying the Bible:

- Do you learn anything new about God or Jesus from this passage? (Maybe it's something about how he feels about you, how he feels about a particular issue or sin, or how he wants us to live.)

- Do you learn any general truths about life or human nature from these verses?
- How does this passage make you feel? Why?
- Are there any instructions or commands to obey in this passage?
- Look at the instructions or commands you wrote down. Why do you think God gives us those teachings? How might they protect or benefit us?
- Do these verses help you see anything you need to add to your life or cut out of your life?
- Does anything surprise or confuse you about this passage? Write down any questions you have so you can talk to someone about them or look into them more later.
- Think about the Bible characters you meet in these verses. In what ways do you relate to them?
- Do you see anything you can imitate in a Bible character's life?
- Do you see anything in a Bible character's life that is something you want to avoid—something you *don't* want to do?

MEDITATION AND MEMORIZATION

The word *meditate* sounds intimidating, right? Kind of mystical, even? But meditating on Scripture is a simple, powerful practice that will add a lot to your experience of the Bible. When you find a Scripture that moves you, don't just read it one time, nod your head, and move on. Meditation can help you learn even more from the passage.

Let's say you find a Scripture that inspires or challenges you, and you want to get more out of it. Start by reading it a few times in a row, looking at each individual word. If you have a Bible app, read the same verse in a few different translations. Sometimes a different version will help you uncover a subtle meaning you missed.

Then spend some time digesting the verse slowly, rolling it around in your heart and mind so you can experience and savor the full flavor of it. The way I meditate on Scriptures is similar to the way I eat chocolate. Every night after I put on my pjs, I settle back against the pillows on my bed and indulge in two squares of Ghirardelli dark chocolate filled with sea salt caramel. (Sorry if I just made you drool on your book.) Eating slowly allows me to taste the distinct flavors of the chocolate and the caramel and to fully appreciate each bite. I take a bite and let the chocolate melt and the caramel ooze. After a second or two, the taste buds on the sides of my tongue start doing their "this tastes like heaven" dance.

Meditating on Scripture is kind of like that: you think about a passage one small "bite" at a time. You let it sit in your brain and on your heart, trying to appreciate all the different flavors and subtleties. You take the time to think about it phrase by phrase, even word by word. What does that phrase tell you about God or yourself? What does that one word add to the meaning?

Let's try meditating on one of my lifelines, Ephesians 1:4:

He chose us in him before the creation of the world to be holy and blameless in his sight.

He chose us: He—God—chose us. *Chose* means handpicked. Selected. Wanted. God chose *you.* Out of all the billions of people on earth, he wanted you.

In him: We are chosen in Jesus. Jesus' blood paid the price and paved the path for us to come to him.

Before the creation of the world: Whoa. Now that's deep. Before God set the sun to burn and the planets to spin, he chose you. He knew you were coming, and he just had to have you as his daughter. (Is your heart tingling yet? Mine is!)

To be holy: Holy means set apart for God's special purposes. It means we're different from the world. Our actions, words, and choices are different, because in all things, we seek to honor God.

And blameless: This might be my favorite word in this whole sentence. *Blameless* means guilt-free! Shame-free! Absolutely, positively, without-a-doubt saved, forgiven, and clean. Christians can talk to God with confidence, knowing we are fully loved and accepted. We can walk around this world confident in Christ, happy in Christ, set free from guilt.

Do you see how meditation works? You can take just one small verse, dive deeply into its meaning, and find life-changing treasures hiding inside. This is how your Bible study comes to life!

You can take your meditation a step further by memorizing your lifeline verses. My strategy for memorization is simple. I write the passage on one side of a three-by-five note card and the Scripture reference on the other side. I memorize the verse one phrase at a time, and before I know it, I've learned the whole passage. Every morning before you start reading your Bible, flip through your note cards to review each verse you've memorized—that way they stay fresh in your mind.

Memorization is kind of like playing an instrument or driving a car: when you do it regularly, you get better at it. The more you make yourself memorize things, the more your brain forms new "memorization pathways" that help you to memorize faster and faster.

Want a head start as you look for your own lifelines? Many of the Scriptures you find listed at the end of each chapter are my lifelines—Scriptures I started collecting when I was in high school to help my heart and grow my faith. Maybe some of my favorites will become yours, too. The more time you spend in your Bible, the more verses of your own you will find.

Our feelings change constantly, but God's Word never does. It is consistent, reliable, and always true. When big feelings come knocking on the door of your heart, God's Word can help you decide if it's time to open the door. When your feelings get tangled, God's Word can unravel the knot. When your feelings start swirling toward the stratosphere, God's Word can gently pull them back down to earth.

As Paul wrote,

> We will no longer be immature like children. We won't be
> tossed and blown about by every wind of new teaching.
> We will not be influenced when people try to trick us
> with lies so clever they sound like the truth. Instead,
> we will speak the truth in love, growing in every way
> more and more like Christ, who is the head of his body,
> the church. . . . Let the Spirit renew your thoughts and
> attitudes. Put on your new nature, created to be like
> God—truly righteous and holy.
> EPHESIANS 4:14-15, 23-24, NLT

When life throws you all the feels, God has all the words and all the wisdom you need. When wild winds blow, your lifeline passages can keep you anchored. When emotional storms try to toss you overboard, Scripture can pull you back to safety. Through fire and water, through wind and waves, God's love—and God's Word—will see you through.

FEELING YOUR WAY FORWARD

Journal Prompts

1. Describe a time when a Scripture helped you to make a decision or make a change.
2. In what situation(s) do you need guidance from God's Word?
3. What do you enjoy about reading your Bible? What do you find difficult or intimidating?
4. Begin keeping a list of "lifeline Scriptures"—passages that mean something special to you and help to define your faith and decisions.

Prayer Prompt

Your word is a lamp to guide my feet
   and a light for my path.

PSALM 119:105, NLT

Lifelines

Five Scriptures about choosing God's way over the ways of the world:

1. Psalm 141:4
2. Psalm 73
3. James 4:4-7
4. 1 John 2:15
5. 1 Peter 2:11-12

CHAPTER 6

HANDLING ALL THE FEELS AT HOME

We have a saying in the South: "When Mama ain't happy, ain't nobody happy." Please don't quote that saying to your English teacher—it has like eight grammatical errors. But the point is clear despite the crimes against grammar: when the mother in a house is upset, the whole house knows it. The whole house is upset.

But you know, in my house, I've noticed a related truth: "When the teenage girl ain't happy, ain't nobody happy." This was true when I was the teenage girl in my house. For better or worse, my moods could take over the entire household. If I was happy, everyone knew it, and I could pull them into my joy. If I was unhappy, everyone knew it, and I could drag them into my pain. And now that I have teenagers of my own, that saying is proving true all over again. When one of the Thompson teens experiences big feelings, their emotions are so big they can take over the entire house and transform the mood of the family—for better or worse.

Quiz: Big Feelings Check

How often do you find yourself experiencing these big feelings? Give yourself points based on the scoring chart below, and then add up your total.

	EMOTION	Multiple times a day	Once a day	Occasionally	Rarely
1.	Confident				
2.	Compassionate				
3.	Excited				
4.	Grateful				
5.	Joyful				
6.	Inspired				
7.	Loving				
8.	Overwhelmed				
9.	Sad				
10.	Insecure				
11.	Lonely				
12.	Anxious				
13.	Guilty				
14.	Angry				
	SUBTOTAL				
	TOTAL				

SCORING

Multiple times a day = 3
Once a day = 2
Occasionally = 1
Rarely = 0

KEY

More than 32 = Big feelings play a big part in your daily life. They take up a lot of your attention. How might you be able to channel some of those emotions to benefit others?

22–32 = You have some big feelings, but they aren't taking over your life. Who in your life might you be able to bless with your balanced approach to emotions?

Fewer than 22 = Big feelings only show up every so often. Which emotions would you like to experience more often?

As we talk about dealing with our emotions at home, let's start by remembering that not all big feelings are bad! Some of our big feelings are a great blessing to our family. My mom used to say that the minute I walked in the door, a sibling party would start. I'd start cracking jokes with my younger brothers and amping my baby sister up on sugar, and before you knew it, we'd all be on the living room floor laughing our heads off. Other times I brought home my big feelings of affection and gratitude. I love *hard*. If I get caught up in a warm-fuzzy fit of *you're-my-favorite-person-ever*, I'm going to tell you, and you're going to feel like the greatest person in the universe.

I bet you have emotional gifts to share at home too. Maybe you're thoughtful and kind or sensitive and intuitive. Maybe you're joyful and funny or creative and expressive. Whatever your emotional gifts, I urge you to share them with your family—don't just keep them to yourself or reserve them for your friendships. Your family needs your gifts too!

But what about the more difficult big feelings, like sadness, insecurity, loneliness, anxiety, or being overwhelmed? What do we do when those big feelings catch us by surprise? How can we deal with them in ways that are healthy?

Let's talk about a few qualities that will help your big feelings remain a blessing to your family. They are selflessness, self-awareness, and self-control.

SELFLESSNESS

Selflessness is at the heart of the Christian faith. Jesus calls us to a life devoted first to God and then to others. Paul describes that life, and the example Jesus set for us, like this:

> Don't be selfish; don't try to impress others. Be humble, thinking of others as better than yourselves. Don't look

out only for your own interests, but take an interest in others, too.

You must have the same attitude that Christ Jesus had.

Though he was God,
    he did not think of equality with God
    as something to cling to.
Instead, he gave up his divine privileges;
    he took the humble position of a slave
    and was born as a human being.
When he appeared in human form,
    he humbled himself in obedience to God
    and died a criminal's death on a cross.

PHILIPPIANS 2:3-8, NLT

Jesus' life was completely devoted to honoring God and serving people. Think about how Jesus spent his time: preaching and teaching, loving and healing. Jesus was often surrounded by a crowd clamoring for his help, begging him for healing. It must have been exhausting, and yet he gave and gave. He did make time to go to quiet places by himself to pray and recharge, but he consistently put others' needs before his own.

When strong feelings barge through the door of my heart, selflessness is one of my biggest challenges. When I'm experiencing big feelings, it's hard to make room in my thoughts for other people. All I can think about is whatever emotion has hijacked my heart and mind.

That's why a story in Matthew 14 (the account of Jesus' response to the death of his friend John the Baptist) consistently inspires and challenges me. It also exemplifies some of the qualities I most admire in Jesus.

John the Baptist was not only a powerful preacher; he was also

Jesus' relative and friend. John was one of the only people who understood who Jesus was and what he had come to do. I have often wondered if, with John out there preaching, perhaps Jesus didn't feel so alone. But John's preaching angered Herod, the local ruler, and John was thrown into jail. Herod's vindictive wife conspired to have John killed, and he was beheaded in prison. Let's pick up the story there:

> Later, John's disciples came for his body and buried it. Then they went and told Jesus what had happened.
> As soon as Jesus heard the news, he left in a boat to a remote area to be alone. But the crowds heard where he was headed and followed on foot from many towns.
> MATTHEW 14:12-13, NLT

When Jesus heard the news about John's death, he needed to be alone. Perhaps he planned to spend a few days mourning and praying. I relate to this part of the story: when I'm sad, I want to be alone. I need time by myself to process and pray. But in other ways, Jesus is radically different from me.

I'm going to retell the story the way I imagine it (see Matthew 14:13-21).

> As the boat nears the dock, Peter springs up onto the wooden slats. His brother, Andrew, tosses him a rope, and Peter ties the rope onto a post, looping it into a knot with expert hands. Peter casts a glance at the sun, now bright and full as a golden coin.
> "A few hours till lunchtime," he says to Jesus. "We'll find a place for you to walk and pray in private until then."
> Jesus and the Twelve all hear it at the same time, coming from behind the tall grasses that line the shore: voices.

Lots of voices, chattering and laughing. And the sound of running feet.

All at once, people spill out from behind the grass at the water's edge. So. Many. People.

Peter mutters under his breath and throws the rope to the ground a little harder than necessary. "How'd they find us here?" He points an accusing finger at Andrew. "Did you tell anyone where we were going?"

Andrew raises his palms. "It wasn't me! I didn't tell!"

Peter claps his brother on the back and then turns to Jesus. "Don't worry, Lord, we'll send them away. You just stay in the boat. If I can't get them to leave, we'll push back out and find another place to . . . Lord? What are you doing?"

Jesus is clambering out of the boat, squinting toward the approaching crowd. He gives Peter a smile. "It's okay, brother. Let them come." Jesus stretches his arms and rolls his head around, as if he's sore from the boat ride. "I rested on the boat. I will preach to these people."

"But Lord." Peter waves an arm at a group of men struggling to carry someone on a wooden pallet. "It's not just preaching they want. They'll want healing too, and you know how much energy that takes—"

Jesus claps Peter on the shoulder. "I know, Peter. It's fine. This is what God has sent me to do."

Jesus turns to the men on the boat and claps his hands. "What's everyone waiting for? James, John, go find a place for the crowd to sit. Thomas, Simon, get the sick lined up as usual so I can heal them."

The Twelve swap surprised looks for a moment, then spring into motion.

Peter sighs. "It's going to be a long day."

Jesus gives him a smile. "It's going to be a *great* day."

Matthew 14 tells us that Jesus spent the entire day preaching and healing, and when evening came, his disciples encouraged him to send the crowd away to get some food. Surely now that it was nearing nightfall, Jesus would give himself a break and get some rest, right?

Wrong.

That evening Jesus did one of his most prominent miracles, feeding thousands of people from a boy's lunch. Only then, after the crowd had had their spiritual and physical fill, did Jesus send them away.

Here we see a stunning example of Jesus' selflessness. Jesus must have been feeling sad about John, perhaps processing the knowledge that his own death was soon to come, but he was able to set that aside for a time so he could give to people who needed him.

But wait. Does that mean we shouldn't deal with our feelings or give ourselves time to deal with sadness? No, that's not what we learn from Jesus. Take a look at what he did that night:

> Immediately after [the evening meal], Jesus insisted that his disciples get back into the boat and cross to the other side of the lake, while he sent the people home. After sending them home, he went up into the hills by himself to pray. Night fell while he was there alone.
>
> Meanwhile, the disciples were in trouble far away from land, for a strong wind had risen, and they were fighting heavy waves. About three o'clock in the morning, Jesus came toward them, walking on the water. When the disciples saw him walking on the water, they were terrified. In their fear, they cried out, "It's a ghost!"

But Jesus spoke to them at once: "Don't be afraid,"
he said. "Take courage. I am here!"

MATTHEW 14:22-27, NLT

Jesus *did* take the time he needed to think and feel and pray.
He took it that night on the mountaintop and then on the water
as he walked to the boat. (Now *that's* how you take a prayer walk!)
We learn from Jesus that when we experience big feelings, we need
to pay attention to both our own needs and the needs of others.
This is true selflessness—the ability to look past the fog of our
own feelings and realize, *Yes, I'm going through something, but other
people have needs too. And God can use me to give to others even when
I don't feel like it.*

Here's a secret that can help us in our quest to become more
selfless: Jesus' consistent prayer life helped him be prepared to
push through and give, even in difficult times. Jesus didn't run on
empty spiritually. He didn't wait for hardship to strike before he
turned to God; he consistently took time away to pray, often early
in the morning or late at night, and those prayer times kept him
filled with spiritual energy (see Mark 1:35; Luke 5:16). When hard
times came unexpectedly, like the day he lost his friend and then
faced a crowd clamoring for his attention, Jesus already had a full
tank to draw from. A consistent prayer life can give us the strength
and energy we need when we're called to be selfless.

SELF-AWARENESS

Self-awareness is the ability to recognize what we're feeling, what
we need, and how we come across to others. In the story we just
read, Jesus was aware of his need to mourn John's death, so he gave
himself the time and space to do so. Yes, he altered his plans when
people needed him, but he still took the time he needed.

Jesus' half-brother James encourages us to take a good look in the mirror to consider who we are and how we need to grow:

> Don't just listen to God's word. You must do what it says. Otherwise, you are only fooling yourselves. For if you listen to the word and don't obey, it is like glancing at your face in a mirror. You see yourself, walk away, and forget what you look like. But if you look carefully into the perfect law that sets you free, and if you do what it says and don't forget what you heard, then God will bless you for doing it.
>
> JAMES 1:22-25, NLT

Self-awareness means that we know ourselves. We know how we respond when we feel sad or insecure or fill-in-the-blank. Each of us responds to big feelings in our own way. Some big feelers may be tempted to blow up or be dramatic. Other big feelers may be tempted to withdraw and sit alone in their hard feelings, staying stuck in a dark place. Reluctant feelers may be tempted to ignore their own emotions (or disregard other people's). Later they're caught off guard when those emotions build up and suddenly explode. Steady feelers may stuff their emotions to avoid the discomfort of feeling upset, but they may find that those ignored feelings leak out in the form of impatience and irritability.

One of my daughters recently had an "off" afternoon. For a half hour or so, she became what our family affectionately calls a Grumpasaurus Rex. (Props to my brother Jonathan for making up this term when we were kids. Okay, maybe it sounds like we're in kindergarten, but, well, it works.)

She was sitting on the couch texting some friends, and her brother had the gall to come into the room eating a bowl of cereal.

"Stop chewing so loud!" she growled, not looking up from her phone.

Two minutes later, to no one in particular, she moaned, "I'm hungry! There's nothing to eat in this house."

Overhearing her complaint from the kitchen, I said, "Sweetie, I can think of at least twelve different snacks in the house: apples, carrots, pineapple, fig bars, peanut butter crackers, Goldfish—"

She cut me off. "Gross. I don't like any of those."

I raised my eyebrows. "Well, that's what we have." I went back to washing potatoes.

She put down her phone for a moment, threw her head back, and groan-shouted at the ceiling. "I'm so bored! I miss my friends!"

Two minutes later, her sister came and sat on the couch beside her. The Grumpasaurus immediately began to complain: "Don't touch me! Stop wiggling! You smell! Go sit somewhere else!"

Hearing this from the kitchen, I put down my scrub brush and walked into the room. "Um, time-out. Do you realize you're barking at everyone in the family?"

She shrugged. Her eyes ping-ponged from me to her phone to me and back to her phone.

"So . . . I think you are feeling frustrated about not getting to hang out with your friends this week, and it's, uh, oozing out all over the rest of us."

She thought for a minute. A sheepish grin tugged at the edge of her mouth. "Yep. That's exactly what I'm doing. Sorry. I'll try to stop."

Being self-aware and naming her feelings helped my daughter change her behavior. She was able to realize that her siblings weren't really being all that annoying (at least, no more annoying than usual); she was just frustrated about other things. Her frustration was pouring out of her in irritability, inflexibility, and harsh words.

How do you act when you feel sad? Frustrated? Insecure? Guilty? What are your go-to reactions, and what oozes out when you aren't paying attention?

- Maybe you become prickly and irritable. (All three feeling types may give in to this one.)
- Or maybe you become weepy and melodramatic, blowing your problems waaaaaaay out of proportion: "My whole life is falling apart! Everything is awful! I have no friends—everyone hates me, including God! I will never be okay again!" *Collapses in a heap on the floor.* (This is a classic big feeler response, though steadies and reluctants can have their Drama Queen moments too.)
- Maybe you become bossy and demanding. (Any feeling type may put on their bossy pants, but this reaction is probably most tempting for steady feelers, who like to find solutions to problems.)
- Maybe you become quiet and withdrawn, hiding from the world in your room. (This is most often a steady or reluctant feeler response, though some big feelers might do it too: first they have a dramatic collapse, then they retreat to their cave.)
- Maybe you lose yourself in distractions, zoning out on your computer or phone, ignoring people. (Private brooding—a classic reluctant feeler response.)

Being aware of your usual reactions to stress is a crucial step in taking charge of the way you act. When I hear myself beginning to think dramatic thoughts like *Everything is horrible,* that's a warning sign. It signals that my emotions are starting to run away from me, and it's time to take control of my feelings before they take control of me.

We start becoming self-aware by doing two things:

- Identifying our warning signs
- Naming our feeling(s)

From there we have to realize that unkind or dramatic responses are not the solution to our feelings—they only make things worse and end up hurting our family and friends and pushing them away.

SELF-CONTROL

Scripture urges us to embrace self-control and gives us some practical tips for doing so:

> Prepare your minds for action and exercise self-control. Put all your hope in the gracious salvation that will come to you when Jesus Christ is revealed to the world. . . . Therefore, be earnest and disciplined in your prayer.
>
> 1 PETER 1:13; 4:7, NLT

Self-control is a fruit of the Holy Spirit's work in our lives (see Galatians 5:22-23). What is self-control? It's the ability to say no to sin and yes to God. It's when we have enough control over our thoughts and emotions that we *remain* in control of them.

For example, self-control means several things:

- When you're in a bad mood, you may feel like making a snide comment to your sibling or friend, but self-control helps you bite your tongue.
- When your parent doesn't understand something you've already explained fifteen times, you may feel like snapping at them, but self-control helps you speak kindly instead.

- When you're angry at a friend who hurts your feelings, you may feel like retaliating—posting something snarky on her social media feed or talking behind her back—but self-control helps you to remain calm and kind in the moment and eventually seek resolution.
- When you feel depressed, you may feel like binge-watching your favorite show, but self-control helps you to find a healthier balance.
- When you feel curious about sex, you may feel like watching something inappropriate on your phone, but self-control helps you to say no—and maybe talk about questions and temptations with a trusted mentor.
- When you feel frustrated by your parents' rules, you may feel like slamming a door and withdrawing, but self-control helps you talk about your frustrations in a calm, respectful way.

We don't master self-control in a day. It's something we work on for our entire lives. I've been a Christian for well over half my life, and I'm still working on self-control, especially when big feelings come into play. When a storm of big feelings starts brewing, I still have to breathe deeply, write down what I'm feeling, and take time to pray and process. I still have to bite my tongue so I don't say things I'll regret—and sometimes I have to apologize when I don't bite hard enough.

Here are a few tricks that can help you reclaim self-control even when big feelings start flying:

- Take a time-out. Remember time-outs from when you were little? They actually work at any age! Give yourself a few minutes alone to calm down, think, and pray.

- Read or recite one of your lifeline Scriptures. If you're feeling angry, a Scripture like Proverbs 15:1 can remind you how to respond in a godly way: "A gentle answer deflects anger, but harsh words make tempers flare" (NLT).
- Take your dramatic thoughts and reframe them. For example:

IF YOU'RE THINKING . . .	REFRAME THAT THOUGHT TO . . .
Nothing in my life ever goes right.	Well, some things in my life are going right, like . . . (Make yourself list three to five positive things to give you a more positive—and realistic—perspective.)
No one loves me. I'm all alone.	I may feel lonely today, but I do have people who love me, including . . . (List a few friends, family members, and mentors.) And even when I don't feel loved by people, I know that God loves me.
I'm a terrible Christian.	I make mistakes as a Christian, but Jesus' blood is more powerful than my sins, and God's grace is huge.

See how that works? When we reframe our thoughts and feelings in light of the truth, it helps slow the swirl before it builds into a full-blown hurricane, and it allows us to regain emotional self-control.

Selflessness, self-awareness, and self-control: three qualities that will help you find more happy in your life, especially at home. And this isn't just for your own life—you'll have more happy to share with others, too.

ALL THE COMPLICATED FAMILY FEELS

Of course, we all want our home lives to be full of joy and love all the time. But they aren't, are they? Family can be complicated. Maybe you've always longed to have a "perfect" family, but the family you have is far messier than the one you imagined. Maybe you've felt the loss of an absent parent or watched your parents struggle in their marriage. Maybe you've experienced a death or divorce in your family or struggled to accept a new stepparent or stepsibling. But please know this: no family is perfect. Every family has cracks and scars. Even Christian families experience tremendous difficulties and heartache: conflict, mental illness, abuse, separation, divorce, remarriage, addiction—the list could go on and on. Family can be complicated and messy, even for godly people.

Know that God is with you even when your family lets you down. Know that God sees—and cares about—whatever hurts and disappointments you face. Know that you can be a powerful woman of God even when you come from brokenness at home. In fact, that brokenness may become part of the way God uses you. God can use your story to give others hope, and he can use the compassion and strength you cultivate through hardship to comfort and guide others who are hurting one day. (But if you feel unsafe or mistreated in some way at home—and abuse can be verbal, emotional, physical, or sexual—please, please, please talk to an adult you can trust: a family member, a minister, a school counselor, a trusted friend. Know that God cares about your suffering, and he wants to give you the help you need.)

Even if your family isn't suffering from some Big Terrible Thing, you may still have some tough dynamics to work through. Over a lifetime together, family relationships can collect a lot of painful baggage, including bad habits of speech and ways of treating each other. When we don't get along with a sibling or parent, it hurts. We may have deep wounds from awful things they've said or done. (And perhaps we have inflicted some wounds on others too.)

When it comes to everyday family conflict, what can we do? How do you handle someone who's really difficult to get along with? Maybe they're a big feeler and their emotions dictate the mood of the house. Or maybe you have a personality conflict and you disagree on—uh, everything. Or maybe you have resentments built up from years of misunderstanding. Or maybe this particular family member just drives you crazy for a million dumb reasons: the way they chew their food; the way they leave their stuff all over the bathroom; the way they borrow your stuff without asking.

Let's talk about the choices we have in our attitudes and behaviors at home. Whenever we struggle to get along with a particular person, here's a hard truth each of us has to accept: *The only person I can change is myself.*

When I was fifteen and my little sister was four—well, let's say she reached a particularly annoying stage. (Sorry, Alexandra. You know I adore you.) It typically went something like this:

* * *

I shut the door to my tiny bedroom. My friend Sara sprawls across the end of my bed, and I settle against the headboard, hugging a pillow. "So," I say, "I really want to hear about yesterday with—"

The door swings open, and there's my little sister, standing in the doorway in her Halloween costume. She beams at Sara and strikes a pose, hands on hips. "Do you like my costume? I'm a bride!"

Sara offers Alexandra a smile. "I do like it! You look beautiful."

Alexandra grabs her skirts and swishes them back and forth. "If I twirl, it poofs! Let me show you!" She twirls and flops on the ground. The dress, which is getting too small (since Halloween was four months ago) doesn't really poof. Sara claps; I roll my eyes.

"Okay, Alexandra, that's enough. Sara and I need some time alone to talk, okay?"

Heaving a sigh, Alexandra walks out, leaving the door gaping open.

"Close the door!" I say, unable to keep the aggravation out of my voice.

Alexandra fumbles with the doorknob and closes the door slowly. Very. Very. Slowly.

"Sorry," I say to Sara.

"It's fine—she's cute. I wish I had a sister."

"So, back to your story," I say. "What happened with the—"

Knock, knock. "Sissy-biss?" My sister's silly nickname for me sounds muffled. I can tell her lips are pressed up against the crack in the door.

I flash Sara an irritated, I'm-sorry-this-keeps-happening smile. "What do you need, Alexandra?"

"Can you play Chutes and Ladders with me?"

"Not right now."

"When?"

"I don't know. Not now. Give us some privacy." My voice sounds really annoyed, so I tack on, "Please." But the *please* sounds even more annoyed than the sentence did.

Three minutes later, the door bursts open. I whirl around to find Alexandra framed in the doorway again. She's making that trying-too-hard-to-be-cute face and holding up her doll and a toy bottle.

"This is Bella," she says to Sara. "She wants you to feed her."

I launch myself off the bed, put my hands on Alexandra's shoulders, twirl her around, and usher her into the hallway, pulling the door shut behind us. "Alexandra," I hiss, "you have to stop interrupting us! Sara didn't come over here to play with you—she came over to hang out with *me*! Now please, go away and leave us alone!"

My sister's bridal shoulders slump, and her hopeful face crumples. She doesn't say anything, just gives a defeated nod. She turns to shuffle down the hallway, dragging poor Bella by the ankle. And I realize: I've seen this view of my sister's back too many times lately. I'm always sending her away.

Standing outside my bedroom, I feel shame and regret barreling through my heart, chasing away my anger. Clarity punches me in the gut. First: *It's not wrong for me to want privacy with my friend, but I don't have to be mean about it.* Then: *I get to choose the kind of big sister I want to be. And I don't like the big sister I've been lately.*

* * *

I couldn't change how little my sister was and how huge our age gap was. I couldn't change her maturity level—yeah, she was going through a slightly annoying phase, but she would grow out of it. I couldn't control everything she did or said. The only thing I could control was the way I responded to her.

In that moment, I made some decisions: *I'm going to be interested in Alexandra's little-girl life even if it's nothing like my high school life. I'm going to be a sister who is willing to play ridiculous games even if they make me look ridiculous too. I want to welcome her into my life—and sometimes even my bedroom—instead of always shutting her out.*

That standing-in-the-hallway-decision was one of the best choices I've ever made. From that day on, things were different between me and Alexandra—because *I* was different. It's not that our relationship suddenly became perfect overnight—she still barged into my room and bugged me, and she needed to learn to give me some space; sometimes I got irritated and had to apologize for being impatient—but the overall feel of our relationship was different. I tried to be more generous, patient, and selfless. We started having "sister days" when we ate junk food and did silly things together. As I worked on giving Alexandra more attention, somehow it helped her to be less pushy and give me more privacy. Somewhere along the way—I couldn't tell you when—that little four-year-old tagalong grew up to be my best friend.

The good news is, it's never too late to start making changes in our relationships. You may not become BFFs with your siblings or parents—sometimes the wounds run too deep or the other person doesn't want (or isn't capable of) the kind of closeness you long for—but we can pray and work toward growth over time.

Yes, families can be complicated, with years of history and hurt, but we have to start somewhere if we want things to be different. Are there changes you can make to set a new course in a relationship? Can you choose different ways of thinking, speaking, or acting? Can you ask for forgiveness? Trust more? Give more? Relationships are difficult—but they're worth it.

My dad always used to say, "Who you are at home is who you really are." (I know. It's a scary truth, right?) So whether you tend to be a Drama Queen, a Grumpasaurus Rex, or a Private Brooder, there's hope for you—there's hope for us all. Let's ask God to help us honor him in who we are at home. Let's practice selflessness, self-awareness, and self-control, knowing that as we work on ourselves, God is working too.

FEELING YOUR WAY FORWARD

Journal Prompts

1. How do you respond when big feelings take over?
2. What are your warning signs that an emotional storm is coming? What actions, words, or moods can tip you off that you need to make some changes?
3. Which of the three characteristics do you want to focus on cultivating: selflessness, self-awareness, or self-control?
4. How would your family members describe you? How would your friends describe you? If the two descriptions are different, why are they different?
5. If you could change one thing about who you are at home, what would you like to change? How might you take a first step toward making that change?

Prayer Prompt

> I will sing of your love and justice, Lord.
> I will praise you with songs.
> I will be careful to live a blameless life—
> when will you come to help me?
> I will lead a life of integrity
> in my own home.

PSALM 101:1-2, NLT

Lifelines

Five Scriptures about selflessness, self-awareness, and self-control:

1. Philippians 2:3-6
2. 1 Corinthians 10:24
3. Matthew 7:12
4. Titus 2:11-13
5. 2 Peter 1:5-7

CHAPTER 7

HOW GOD FEELS ABOUT YOU

Have you ever walked through one of those super-creepy and not-fun-at-all "fun houses" at the fair where you look in all the weird mirrors? One makes you look short and round; another makes you look tall and lean; another distorts your features till you look like that famous *Scream* painting.

Insecurity can warp the mirror of your self-image, making you see yourself every way but how you truly are. It magnifies your weaknesses and minimizes your strengths.

This is a little like the way we see ourselves without God's Word to guide our vision. When we look at ourselves with our own worldly, insecure eyes, we can't see things as they truly are. We may *think* we're seeing clearly, but our eyes are magnifying the wrong things—all our pimples and crooked parts, our weaknesses and sins.

Maybe someone who loves you has tried to tell you who you really are in Christ, how you really look to God—"You are beautiful, dearly loved, richly gifted"—but you couldn't see it for yourself. You couldn't believe the truth.

When we learn to see ourselves through the mirror of the Bible—the way our Father sees us—our vision becomes clear. It is true.

And in Christ we are beautiful.

If you had asked me to describe myself in high school, my list would have gone something like this:

I am . . .

- not hideous, but not especially pretty;
- smart but disorganized;
- a procrastinator;
- rhythmically challenged (translation: a horrible dancer);
- too insecure to be cool;
- a mediocre athlete;
- not funny;
- a deep feeler (aka too sensitive);
- a deep thinker (aka nerdy);
- a devoted but jealous friend;
- selfish;
- prideful.

I know. My list is overwhelmingly negative, isn't it? It took years before I finally realized that I couldn't trust my own analysis of myself. My mind's "mirror" wasn't giving me an accurate reflection.

And you know what else I realized? My self-analysis wasn't the one that mattered. What mattered then—what matters now—is how *God* sees me. And the same holds true for you. It doesn't matter what the world thinks of you—it doesn't even matter what *you* think of you. What matters is how God sees you.

Of course, we all have a sinful nature, and that part of us—the person we are without Christ—is not good. Not beautiful. As Paul describes it, "There is no one righteous, not even one. . . . For all have sinned and fall short of the glory of God" (Romans 3:10, 23). We all have a sin problem, and we all need Jesus to forgive us and transform our sin problem, to help us become the people God always meant for us to be. But many of us have another ongoing problem: even after we become Christians, we struggle to accept our new identity. We have a hard time seeing ourselves through the mirror of grace and forgiveness.

So what does God see when he looks at you?

WHO GOD SAYS YOU ARE

As a Christian who has been forgiven through the blood of Jesus, this is who you are to God:

You are blameless.

> He chose us in him before the creation of the world to be holy and blameless in his sight.
>
> EPHESIANS 1:4

Blameless means having no guilt. No sin. It has all been washed away. When you become a Christian, you can stand confidently before God, thanks to the sacrifice of his Son.

You are never forgotten.

> Can a mother forget her nursing child?
>   Can she feel no love for the child she has borne?
> But even if that were possible,
>   I would not forget you!
> See, I have written your name on the palms of my hands.
>
> ISAIAH 49:15-16, NLT

You are always on God's mind. He knows what you need before you even ask (see Matthew 6:8). He could never forget you.

You are forgiven.

> In him we have redemption through his blood, the
> forgiveness of sins, in accordance with the riches of God's
> grace that he lavished on us.
>
> EPHESIANS 1:7-8

Jesus' blood doesn't work halfway or only part of the time. You are forgiven for everything you've ever done or ever will do. You are forgiven even when you're in the middle of a mess. And God doesn't hand out stingy rations of forgiveness, like, *You'd better be careful with this—when it runs out, you'll be on your own.* God's forgiveness is as vast as the ocean. He will give you second chances, third chances, thirty millionth chances if you need them.

You are understood and known.

> You have searched me, LORD,
>   and you know me.
> You know when I sit and when I rise;
>   you perceive my thoughts from afar.
> You discern my going out and my lying down;
>   you are familiar with all my ways.
> Before a word is on my tongue
>   you, LORD, know it completely.
> You hem me in behind and before,
>   and you lay your hand upon me.
>
> PSALM 139:1-5

Other people don't always see the real you. People don't know your every thought. People can't grasp your every feeling. But God can—he can, and he does.

You are his beloved child.

> I have cared for you since you were born.
>> Yes, I carried you before you were born.
> I will be your God throughout your lifetime—
>> until your hair is white with age.
> I made you, and I will care for you.
>> I will carry you along and save you.

ISAIAH 46:3-4, NLT

Maybe you don't know your earthly father or mother, or maybe your relationship is difficult, complicated, or strained. You ache to feel love, approval, and adoration from your earthly parents. If that has been your experience, I ache with you and for you. Maybe there's a hole in your heart where all that love should be. But believe it or not, there's someone who wants to step in and flood that hole so full of love it spills out all over the place: God.

As we draw out this idea of God's fatherly love in this chapter and throughout this book, I'm going to write about a few memories of my earthly father. I share these moments not to make you feel sad if you aren't close to your dad but to help paint a picture of God as your perfect Father—and all the beautiful ways he loves you. If you've never seen a loving father in action, it can be difficult to wrap your brain around what it means for God to be your heavenly Father. I hope these stories help to fill in that picture for you and help you accept and enjoy the heart-filling, soul-healing love of your Dad in heaven.

God wants to walk beside you and hold your hand, even though you're too old for it. He wants to take you to work with him and show you off to his friends. He wants to jump around on the sidelines cheering when you play sports (even if you're terrible). He wants to hear All the Things about your day—even the things no one else seems to care about. That's the love your heavenly Father has for you.

You are wanted, sought after.

> If a man has a hundred sheep and one of them wanders away, what will he do? Won't he leave the ninety-nine others on the hills and go out to search for the one that is lost? And if he finds it, I tell you the truth, he will rejoice over it more than over the ninety-nine that didn't wander away! In the same way, it is not my heavenly Father's will that even one of these little ones should perish.
>
> MATTHEW 18:12-14, NLT

God never stops seeking you, running after you. If everyone else is safe and happy but you're not, you can be sure he'll leave the pack and go on a desperate search. And when he finds you, he'll let out a celebratory whoop, put you on his strong shoulders, and carry you home.

WHERE YOUR VIEW OF YOURSELF COMES FROM

It can be tempting to let other people define us and our worth. If you're a big feeler, you might try to get your worth from how your relationships are going from day to day. You may feel confident only when you feel deeply connected to other people. If you're a steady feeler, you might be tempted to find your worth in proving that you're capable and inspiring—you don't want to risk showing emotional "weakness." If you're a reluctant feeler, you might draw confidence from your reputation as a strong, independent person who doesn't care what people think. But what about the times when you don't feel strong or when you get hurt? All these responses are false measures of our identity.

- Your view of yourself can't come from other people.
- It can't come from your accomplishments.
- It can't come from your appearance.
- It can't come from who you're dating.
- It can't come from your friendships.
- It can't come from your reputation.
- It can't come from the number of friends or fans you have on social media.
- It can't come from your likes, comments, or followers.

None of those things is permanent or reliable. Only God is permanent and reliable. Here we can learn from Jesus. Even when people were saying all kinds of wonderful things about him, Jesus didn't pay attention.

> Now while he was in Jerusalem at the Passover Festival, many people saw the signs he was performing and believed in his name. But Jesus would not entrust himself to them, for he knew all people. He did not need any testimony about mankind, for he knew what was in each person.
> JOHN 2:23-25

It's a good thing Jesus didn't depend on people for his self-image, because at other times in his life, people said horrible things about him. Take a look at some of the accusations people threw at him:

- He was a liar (see John 6:41-42).
- He was demon possessed (see Mark 3:22).
- He was a blasphemer—someone who shows total disrespect for God (see Luke 5:21).
- He was a drunk (see Matthew 11:19).
- He was friends with the wrong crowd (see Matthew 11:19).

If Jesus had depended on people for his self-image, he would have lost all confidence in who God had called him to be. Our confidence can't come from people, who are ever changing and don't always speak what's true. Our confidence comes from God, who never changes and is always honest.

GOD-ESTEEM, NOT SELF-ESTEEM

You might think the message of this chapter is: You're awesome! Be confident in who God made you to be! And it is, sort of . . . but it's more than that. The point isn't to work on your self-image; it's to see yourself as *God* sees you. To get your identity from God, not from yourself.

Because here's the crazy thing, the thing that will make your neurons explode if you think about it for too long: God's love for you doesn't depend on you. It doesn't depend on your actions. It doesn't depend on your performance.

You don't have to earn God's love—in fact you *can't* earn it.

You don't have to prove yourself worthy. Through Jesus, you are already worthy. He is worthy . . . and therefore you are worthy.

You don't have to maintain a certain level of performance in order to remain in God's love.

- God loves you even though you're imperfect and sinful (see Romans 5:8).
- God loves you even while you're stumbling around making a mess of things (see Psalm 51:7-12).
- God loves you even if you make huge mistakes or try to push him away (see Psalm 32:1-5).
- You can't talk him out of loving you (see Luke 15:21-24).
- You can't sin your way out of his love. Sin hurts us and sin hurts God, but even when we sin, God never

stops loving us or trying to win our hearts back (see Jeremiah 24:7).

- God loves you even if people—maybe your own family members—have made you feel unworthy (see Psalm 27:10).
- You can't hide from God. He will find you even in the darkness. Running from him won't make him give up on you. He will wait for you. Even if we try to leave God, he never leaves us (see Psalm 139:7-12).

Does that mean we can sin and live however we want? Does grace mean we take advantage of God's kindness and live like, *Whatever. I can do anything I want because God loves me?* Of course not! God's grace inspires us to love him back. It's like having a close friendship—you treat your friend well because you respect her and value the relationship. You don't talk about her behind her back because you care about her and don't want to do anything to jeopardize the trust you've built.

God's grace doesn't mean it doesn't matter if we sin. Sin often has consequences that hurt us (or other people), and it's always better if we stay away from it. And we deeply appreciate the sacrifice Jesus made to purchase our forgiveness, so we strive to honor his gift with the way we live. But God doesn't give up on us when we make mistakes. He doesn't stop loving us just because we've made a mess—or are still in the middle of a mess—trying to find our way back to him.

HOW DOES THIS CHANGE YOU?

When you know how much God loves you—when you let that love warm you from the inside, seeping into your bones, strengthening your heart, easing your fears, comforting your hurts—it changes everything.

It changes the way you think—and feel—about yourself.

- You are confident.
- You know that you are valuable.
- You know that you are lovable.
- You know that you are likable.
- Guilt fades, and gratitude takes its place: *I don't deserve all this, but wow, I'm so grateful!*

It changes the way you feel about friendships.

- Friendships are great, and you enjoy having them, but you don't depend on friends for your sense of worth.
- Your happiness isn't determined by your popularity. In each friendship, you recognize that you have something to give.

It changes the way you live.

- You obey God out of love and the desire to make him happy, not out of guilt or duty.
- You read your Bible and pray because you love spending time with your Father—hearing what he has to say, telling him all that's on your heart, and sharing life with him.
- You offer kindness and forgiveness to others because God has shown kindness and forgiveness to you.

It changes the way you feel about guys.

- You don't need a boyfriend to give you confidence and make you feel loved and valuable, because you already know you're loved by your Father.
- You are willing to wait for a Christian guy who loves you and protects you the way God does.

* * *

Oh, how adored you are, beautiful girl! You are sung over, celebrated, enjoyed. My prayer for you is that you will fully understand how crazy-loved you are. God's love is so big that he has to give us the power to understand it. Our little brains are too weak to grasp the enormity of his feelings for us! I pray that God will continue to expand your brain—and heart—so you can more fully feel his love.

> May you have the power to understand, as all God's people should, how wide, how long, how high, and how deep his love is. May you experience the love of Christ, though it is too great to understand fully. Then you will be made complete with all the fullness of life and power that comes from God.
>
> EPHESIANS 3:18-19, NLT

FEELING YOUR WAY FORWARD

Journal Prompts

1. How do you think God feels about you? In what ways does your answer agree—or disagree—with the Scriptures we read in this chapter?
2. When you think about God's love for you, how does it affect your view of yourself?
3. What's the difference between "God-esteem" and self-esteem?
4. How could a better understanding of God's love change your friendships and your relationships with guys?

Prayer Prompt

> Show me the wonders of your great love,
> you who save by your right hand
> those who take refuge in you from their foes.
> Keep me as the apple of your eye;
> hide me in the shadow of your wings.

PSALM 17:7-8

Lifelines

Five Scriptures about God's love:

1. Exodus 19:4-6
2. Psalm 103:17
3. Psalm 139:7-10
4. Deuteronomy 7:6
5. Deuteronomy 14:2

CHAPTER 8

WHEN YOU CAN'T DEAL

Senior year, February. I'm lying in bed, but sleep is a distant dream. My mind swoops and swirls, a kite in a tornado.

Will I get into Duke?

My GPA is solid. I'm totally getting in.

But I got a C in calculus first quarter. I'm totally not getting in.

Ugh, calculus. I still don't get it. I need to cram hard for next week's test.

All my other grades were As, though. Maybe I'll still get in.

If I don't get into Duke, I will die. Okay, not really, but emotionally.

If I don't get into Duke, will I end up at Emory? In Georgia?

I DON'T EVEN KNOW WHAT STATE I'M GOING TO LIVE IN NEXT YEAR.

If I move to Georgia, will I even know my little sister anymore? Will she remember having me at home? She's only seven—how could I leave her and move so far away?

Will my parents be mad at me if I leave?

Speaking of mad . . . I think Bri is mad at me. She acted weird all day. What did I do wrong? I didn't sit with her at lunch because I didn't feel like being outside—did I hurt her feelings?

I haven't heard from Jack in a month. He's totally moving on. Forgetting me.

Maybe I want him to forget me. Maybe I want to go out with Football Boy instead.

I can't handle the drama.

Drama. I should have taken drama instead of calculus. Why'd I have to give myself such a difficult final semester of high school?

I'm a senior. I'm supposed to be having the time of my life. Why am I miserable?

I. Can't. Handle. My. Life.

I'm so overwhelmed.

*   *   *

Ever been there? Just . . . overwhelmed? Anxious? Teetering on the edge of Panic Mode? Feeling all the feels all at once? No idea how to untangle them or how to calm down? Welcome to the club—I feel your pain.

The amazing news is, God understands what it's like to feel overwhelmed. One of the reasons God sent Jesus to earth was so that he could experience all the feelings we do and relate to us in a been-there, felt-that way. Jesus felt overwhelmed himself on the night he was arrested—so overcome with feelings that he thought he might die from the force of them: "My soul is overwhelmed with sorrow to the point of death," he told his friends Peter, James, and John. "Stay here and keep watch with me" (Matthew 26:38).

And Jesus wasn't the only person in Scripture who felt the weight of strong emotions. God went out of his way to include many examples of people in the Bible who felt overwhelmed. Take a look at this prayer:

Listen to my prayer, O God.
Do not ignore my cry for help!
Please listen and answer me,
for I am overwhelmed by my troubles.

PSALM 55:1-2, NLT

God included examples like these (and many others) because he wants us to know he has compassion for our feelings—even the ginormous ones that feel like tsunamis ready to crash over us and drag us away.

GOD CARES ABOUT YOUR FEELINGS

Let's take a closer look at a time in Scripture when one of our Bible heroes, Elijah, felt overwhelmed, nearly paralyzed by anxiety. Elijah had just experienced one of his most dramatic, mighty moments as a prophet: in an epic showdown, he defeated 850 pagan prophets. The victory was so stunning that news quickly traveled to the ears of the evil queen Jezebel, who immediately sent assassins to hunt Elijah down.

You'd think Elijah's faith would be soaring after his victory, that he'd be totally confident in God's protection and power, that he'd say to Jezebel the ancient equivalent of, "Nanny-nanny, boo-boo, you can't catch me! My God's way more powerful than you!" But nope. Elijah was terrified, and he started running. (Doesn't that make you feel better about those moments when you "should" be confident in God but instead you give in to fear and go into hiding?) Here's what happened:

Elijah was afraid and fled for his life. He went to Beersheba, a town in Judah, and he left his servant there. Then he went on alone into the wilderness, traveling all day. He sat down under a solitary broom tree and prayed that he might die. "I have had enough, LORD," he said. "Take my life, for I am no better than my ancestors who have already died."

Then he lay down and slept under the broom tree. But as he was sleeping, an angel touched him and told him, "Get up and eat!" He looked around and there beside his head was some bread baked on hot stones and a jar of water! So he ate and drank and lay down again.

1 KINGS 19:3-6, NLT

Whew. Does this sound familiar at all? Elijah felt so overwhelmed that he threw himself under a broom tree and gave up, exhausted and hopeless. (Ever tried to sleep away your problems?) If you've ever felt like Elijah did, if you've ever visited the deep, dark places, you can draw comfort from his story.

When Elijah awoke, he came face-to-face with God's eternal goodness. If Elijah could come back from his deep, dark place, so can you. If God helped Elijah to step back into the light, he'll help you too.

Take a look at how kind God was to Elijah when he was feeling fragile. What did God do for Elijah?

- He spoke kindly to him.
- He sent an angel to comfort him.
- He gave him food.
- He encouraged him to rest.

The next time you're feeling overwhelmed with Supersized feelings, remember Elijah and the way God took care of him. You can express your deepest, most difficult feelings to your loving Father, and he will hear you. He will speak tenderly to you through encouraging passages in his Word. (And you might even take a hint from God's advice to Elijah: a good meal and a long nap might take the edge off your feelings!)

Let's step away from Elijah's story for a moment to consider some practical applications.

TIPPING POINTS AND DRAMA QUEENS

Want to know one of the most amazing blessings you have in Christ? You get to work out your feelings with God's help. Like Elijah, you may feel overwhelmed for a time, but you don't have to stay overwhelmed. You may feel stuck, but you don't have to stay stuck. Whether you're a big feeler who uses the word *overwhelmed* as part of your daily vocabulary or a steady or reluctant feeler who only feels that way occasionally, God offers help and hope to all of us!

When I'm feeling overwhelmed, I've found that I have a tipping point—a point of no return. A point where just feeling overwhelmed spirals into something more destructive, like pushing away someone who's trying to help or saying Not Nice Things That I Don't Really Mean or going into Panic Mode, where utter freakout meets snot-flying, chest-heaving sobs. In other words, *drama*.

Now let's clarify: there's nothing wrong with crying—Jesus himself shed tears (see John 11:35 and Hebrews 5:7). And thank goodness God welcomes our tears, because my tear ducts like to get in on the action any time I'm having big feelings. A few months after I got married, my husband teased me, "I never knew I'd married a sprinkler!" (Insert eye roll emoji here.) But we have to remember that there's a difference between processing emotions in a healthy way and allowing our overwhelmed feelings to spin out of control.

If I'm being honest, I usually cross that threshold knowingly. There's a moment when a calm voice in my brain whispers behind all my loud feelings: *Hey, Elizabeth, let's take a time-out. You don't have to go there. You could take a few deep breaths, read the Bible, pray, call a friend—something.*

If I listen to that voice and do what it says, things take a more positive turn. I start calming down. Maybe not in five minutes, but I start heading in the right direction. Within a half hour I feel more like myself, and within an hour I may feel exhausted but calmer. More rational. Less like the world is ending.

If I *don't* listen to that voice, my feelings mushroom like a nuclear cloud ready to poison everyone within a hundred miles.

It's okay to feel overwhelmed for a while. It's okay to cry. It's okay to feel anxious or stressed or upset and have to work your way through the feeling. It's *not* okay to take our feelings out on other people in the form of anger or freak-outs. And it's not okay to use our big feelings as an excuse for sin. As Proverbs 16:32 says, "Better to be patient than powerful; better to have self-control than to conquer a city" (NLT).

That moment the little voice of reason pipes up in the back of your mind, that's the tipping point, the point when you get to decide what happens next. The next time you feel overwhelmed and you're tempted to go to that out-of-control place, I encourage you to listen for that still, calm voice—and do what that voice says.

Now, can we be honest about an embarrassing secret for a second? Lean in closer so I can whisper: Sometimes we sort of like feeling overwhelmed. Sometimes we enjoy feeling—and being— dramatic. Sometimes we tell other people (and ourselves), "I can't help the way I feel. I can't change the way I feel." But deep inside, we know that's not true. Sometimes we don't change because we don't try . . . and because we don't want to change.

We don't like to admit it, but a little Drama Queen lives inside us, and sometimes she enjoys being theatrical. She loves to sneak out of her castle, take center stage, and rage and cry and stomp and make shocking statements that whip everyone around her into a frenzy of worry. She ignores others' feelings and makes the whole world revolve around herself and her feelings; she may even use her emotions as an excuse to intentionally hurt others. She enjoys it when life feels like a tragic movie and she gets to be the star—it feels exciting and oddly romantic!

I know. I just exposed your secret inner Drama Queen. Don't worry—I have one living inside me too. *Shhh.* It can be our little secret. We all have times when we are tempted to let our Drama Queen out to indulge in Big Dramatic Moments, and none of us handles our big feelings well every time. Big feelers, your Drama Queen may be a flashy dresser who carries a bullhorn and makes frequent appearances—just like your feelings. Steadies, your Drama Queen may not show up as often, but she knows how to make a grand entrance. Reluctant feelers, your Drama Queen may be more of the brooding type who slips away and hides from the world in her curtained bed. If anyone dares invade her private space to ask, "What's going on? Are you okay? Are you ever coming out?" she probably snaps at them.

We all respond differently to big feelings. But the more self-aware we become, the better prepared we will be to manage our little Drama Queen when she tries to make an appearance.

Remember, it's okay to feel overwhelmed at times. You may need to remind yourself of this truth, especially if you're a guilty soul who feels bad when you don't feel the "right" way. Elijah is considered one of the greatest prophets, and he experienced a significant season of being utterly overwhelmed and depressed. We should be as gentle with ourselves as God was with Elijah. However, we also have to develop resilience, grow emotionally, and move forward so we can accomplish God's purposes for us. Elijah's story shows us that God can help us so we don't *stay* in that place.

We're talking here about being overwhelmed and down—

feelings we all deal with from time to time. These emotions aren't the same thing as having an anxiety disorder or being clinically depressed. If you've been feeling overwhelmed, hopeless, or down for longer than two weeks and nothing is helping, please talk to someone (a family member, a pastor, a mentor, a trusted friend) and get some help. It might be time to look into counseling or get guidance from a doctor. God has given wisdom to therapists, doctors, counselors, psychologists, and psychiatrists for a reason—please don't be afraid to take advantage of it!

STRATEGIES FOR DEALING WITH OVERWHELMING FEELINGS

When we left Elijah, he was resting under a tree. From there he traveled forty more days and ended up in a cave where, I'm sorry to tell you, he was still upset. His fearful, overwhelmed feelings began tipping toward self-pity and despair. Here's my interpretation of what happened (see 1 Kings 19):

> The voice of God calls into the cave: "What are you doing here, Elijah? Go out and stand before me on the mountain."
>
> Elijah takes a few steps forward—trembling, afraid. *Has God finally had enough of me? Has he run out of patience?* He hesitates for a heartbeat before stepping out of the cave.
>
> Outside, the air swirls and shrieks, a mighty wind. The roar is so loud Elijah cringes, inches back into the cave, and covers his ears. Through the mouth of the cave, he sees boulders breaking free, tumbling down with violent crashes. Elijah's trembling builds till his teeth clang and his knees can hardly hold him up. But then he realizes: *It's not* me *shaking—it's the mountain!*

The shaking slows, though Elijah still feels the echo of it in his wobbly legs and knees. And then a huge fire roars, reaching flaming fingers into the cave till Elijah

Quiz: How Drama Prone Are You?

How often do you say and do the following things? Give yourself points based on the scoring chart below, and then add up your total.

	THINGS I SAY AND DO	Often	Sometimes	Rarely
1.	I make statements that include "always" or "never."			
2.	I become upset when things don't go the way I want them to.			
3.	People tell me to calm down.			
4.	I struggle to see a way out of problems. My problems feel like they're going to last forever.			
5.	I have dramatic disagreements with people.			
6.	When I'm hurt, I react by blowing up or shutting down.			
7.	My mood swings drastically throughout the day.			
8.	My feelings are easily hurt.			
	SUBTOTAL			
	TOTAL			

SCORING
Often = 3
Sometimes = 2
Rarely = 1

KEY
21–24: Your Drama Queen likes to make frequent appearances. When she arrives, take a breath and remind yourself that she doesn't get to call all the shots!
16–20: You've got a decent handle on your Drama Queen, but she sometimes makes a scene. When she does, remind her that your words and actions are ruled by your heart *and* your head.
0–15: Your Drama Queen stays inside her chambers most of the time. It's good to keep the drama low! But be sure you don't stuff those feelings either.

staggers back. As suddenly as it sprang to life, the fire dies. And in the quiet, a gentle whisper calls: *Elijah*.

Elijah knows the Lord is here. He steps out of the cave.

"What are you doing here, Elijah?"

"I have zealously served you, Lord, but your people have abandoned you for foreign gods. They've torn down your altars and killed your prophets! I am the only one left, and they are trying to kill me, too."

God says, "Go back the way you came and anoint a new king. I'm giving you a new partner. By the way, you're wrong—you're not the only righteous person left. I still have seven thousand faithful Israelites!"

* * *

God's response—both loving and honest—helped Elijah step out of the cave and back into life. God helped Elijah to see things as they really were instead of the way he *felt* they were:

- Elijah felt like he was alone, but God knew there were seven thousand other faithful believers nearby.
- Elijah felt hopeless, but God was still with him.
- Elijah felt like giving up, but God still had big plans for his life.

God was able to help Elijah overcome feeling overwhelmed so he could go on to the next thing God was calling him to. Following God doesn't mean we'll never be overwhelmed; it just means he'll give us strategies to cope when we feel that way.

Five Things to Do When You Feel Overwhelmed

Here are a few practical suggestions for when you realize a storm of overwhelmed or anxious feelings is brewing inside you.

1. Write down what you're feeling. Number all the different feelings so you can figure out how many emotions you're actually dealing with. Sometimes I feel like I'm worried about eighteen things, when really I'm just worrying about one thing eighteen different ways.

2. Name your feelings before God. Elijah was only able to work through his overwhelming feelings through conversations with the Lord. When you begin to feel overwhelmed or anxious, take your feelings to God in honest prayer. Tell him what you're feeling and ask him to help you sort through it. Remember, God wants to hear what you're feeling.

I cry out to the LORD;
  I plead for the LORD's mercy.
I pour out my complaints before him
  and tell him all my troubles.
When I am overwhelmed,
  you alone know the way I should turn.
PSALM 142:1-3, NLT

3. Elijah received direct instructions from God's lips. We may not get audible messages from God, but when we want to hear God's voice, we can search the Bible for what he wants to say to us. Open your Bible and find your go-to verses—the lifeline verses we've been talking about.

4. Focus on what you *can* do. When I'm feeling overwhelmed, I like to make a list of simple things I can do. Sometimes the list is ridiculously simple, like:

- Maybe I can't do all thirty-six things on my way-too-long to-do list, but I can put away my laundry and go for a run. That's a start.
- Maybe I can't catch up on all my homework today, but I can do the shortest and easiest assignment so I can cross one thing off the list.
- Maybe I can't figure out all the problems in the friendship I'm worried about, but I can send a nice text and pray that God helps us work things out.

This won't make all your worries go away, but it will help you feel less overwhelmed and anxious. It will release you from being paralyzed and help you start moving forward.

5. Talk to a trusted friend or adviser. Notice that God sent Elijah to hang out with Elisha, a spiritual man who became Elijah's companion and friend. When we're overwhelmed, we need other people. One note: choose your person wisely. This isn't the time to call your friend who loves drama and will feed the fire of your worries. This is the time to talk to your even-keeled friend (steady and reluctant-feeling friends, this is your time to shine!), your youth group leader, a parent, a spiritual mentor— someone who can listen compassionately but also speak truth to your feelings.

JUST LIKE US

Elijah wasn't the only godly person in Scripture who felt over-whelmed. Scripture gives us a lot of stories about men and women just like us who struggled with hard things, feeling like they just couldn't make it, like they just couldn't deal. Yet God saw them through those times. Paul wrote about a time when he and his friends felt overwhelmed:

> We now have this light shining in our hearts, but we ourselves are like fragile clay jars containing this great treasure. This makes it clear that our great power is from God, not from ourselves.
>
> We are pressed on every side by troubles, but we are not crushed. We are perplexed, but not driven to despair. We are hunted down, but never abandoned by God. We get knocked down, but we are not destroyed. Through suffering, our bodies continue to share in the death of Jesus so that the life of Jesus may also be seen in our bodies.
>
> 2 CORINTHIANS 4:7-10, NLT

God saw Paul through his troubles. And Elijah. And Jesus. And countless others who felt overwhelmed just like we do. I suspect one reason our kind Father gave us their stories was to say, *If you will turn to me, I will help you just as I helped them. Like Elijah, you will step out of the cave to live again. Like Paul, you will stand up when you get knocked down. Like Jesus, you'll conquer darkness and claim victory. You can be strong because I am strong. Nothing that overwhelms you overwhelms me. No matter what life throws at you, you can make it—I've got you.*

FEELING YOUR WAY FORWARD

Journal Prompts

1. What makes you feel most overwhelmed? Family troubles? Friend drama? Schoolwork? An uncertain future?

2. How do you usually act when you feel overwhelmed? How would you like to respond when you feel overwhelmed?
3. List one thing you *can* do about something that's currently overwhelming in your life.
4. Describe your inner Drama Queen. What kinds of things does she like to do or say?

Prayer Prompt

O God, listen to my cry!
    Hear my prayer!
From the ends of the earth,
    I cry to you for help
    when my heart is overwhelmed.
Lead me to the towering rock of safety,
    for you are my safe refuge,
    a fortress where my enemies cannot reach me.
Let me live forever in your sanctuary,
    safe beneath the shelter of your wings!

PSALM 61:1-4, NLT

Lifelines

Five Scriptures to read when you're overwhelmed:

1. John 16:33
2. Psalm 46:1-3
3. 2 Corinthians 12:8-10
4. 1 Peter 5:7
5. Psalm 18:2

CHAPTER 9

WHEN FEELINGS CRASH THE FRIENDSHIP PARTY

My daughter is texting a group of friends. "I'm sharing about God," she says, cheeks bright, eyes shining. "Telling them what I really believe and why I became a Christian last summer." She flashes me a nervous but excited grin.

"That's great, honey," I say, looking up from my computer. "I'm so proud of you!"

Five minutes later, she slouches back into the kitchen, face pale, eyes brimming. "Carrie's being so mean. She says I shouldn't talk to the group about God and no one wants to hear it." She takes a sharp breath. "She said I should just shut up. I thought at least Rachel would stand up for me, but she totally left me hanging. She said Carrie's right, and I need to stop pushing my faith on people." She hands me the phone, tears slipping down her cheeks.

* * *

Can we be honest? Friendships—even Christian friendships—can be complicated. Way complicated. When you feel close to a friend and the vibe is flowing and conversation is clicking, the whole world feels sunshiny, hope filled, magical. Life is a musical, and you might just break into a song and dance in the middle of the street. But when things are off with a friendship, the world feels shadowy, scary, uncertain. Life is a conspiracy, and you can't trust anyone. And when you can't find a good friend, or when you lose a friend, the world can feel lonely, frustrating, and snobby. Life is an exclusive party, and you didn't get an invitation.

Friendships can be a source of big feelings, from delightful to devastating and all the feels in between. One day those feelings are a fountain of joy: *Someone knows me, sees me, gets me!* The next day they're a mud pit of misery: *No one sees, no one understands, no one cares.* Friendships can lead us to God or pull us away from him. They can make us stronger Christians or lead us off the path. They can help us become the people God designed us to be, or they can turn us into people we don't even recognize.

FRIENDSHIP MYTHS

There are a lot of myths out there about friendships, and those myths can lead to a lot of big feelings. Let's take a look at a few of the most common myths.

Everyone else has close friendships except me.

You walk into a birthday party, and everyone is already clumped together in pairs and groups. Laughing, whispering, hugging. You hesitate in the doorway, eyes frantically scanning the room for someone—anyone—to talk to, but all the groups are closed circles, with no room for one more. No one waves you over, no one saved you a spot, no one even sees that you're there. You look down, half-wondering if you've turned invisible. Humiliation snakes its clammy fingers around your heart; insecurity slithers into your mind: *What's wrong with me? Why does everyone have friends except me?*

This same scenario happens on social media too. You scroll through your phone and see picture after picture of girls (who apparently never have bad skin or bad hair days) hugging and laughing, looking perfectly chummy and friends-forevery. And the captions! "Besties since kindergarten!" "She's always there for me!" At first you're like, *Aw, how sweet*, but before long you're like, *What's wrong with me? Why wasn't I invited to that party? Why doesn't anyone feel this way about me?*

Here's the thing, though: social media doesn't tell the whole story. People only post what they want other people to see. Nobody posts captions like, "Well, we hang out together a lot and here's a picture of us laughing, but I was actually fake-laughing, and she was kind of being rude that day. She talks about herself all the time and forgets to ask how I'm doing. Sometimes I feel bad about myself when we're together because we gossip. I actually wish I could get out of this 'friendship,' but I don't have anyone else, and I feel trapped. It's better than being alone. So now I'm posting this picture so people think I have friends."

Nope, nobody posts those things.

You have to learn to see through the false projections people put out there. I'm not saying you need to be cynical; I'm not saying all the pictures on social media are insincere. Just don't believe everything you see and everything people say or post. Don't compare your *actual* reality to other people's *social media* reality.

In my years of ministry, I've worked with hundreds of women of all ages: preteens, teens, college students, single women, married women, mothers, and grandmothers. And guess what I've noticed? *Almost every woman wishes she had better friendships.* Almost every woman feels lonely sometimes. Almost every woman sometimes wonders if the rest of the world has BFFs while she's the only one who's left out.

If I don't have good friends, I can't be happy or confident.

I went to three different middle schools and three different high schools. It takes time to build trust and shared memories, and sometimes I just didn't have time to build those before we moved again. You know what I learned to do, because I didn't have another choice? I learned to turn to God as my friend—my first and best and *always* friend. We all have times when our friendships aren't as rich or as plentiful as we want them to be, but as Christians, we have one Friend who is always by our side (see Matthew 28:20).

Friendships just "happen."

It was the summer after ninth grade, somewhere in the mountains of West Virginia. The cramped minivan smelled like french fries. Soon-to-be-a-sophomore-at-another-new-school me stared out the window as the rainy world slipped by, a smear of gray clouds and green trees.

I searched my soul. *I'm tired of being insecure. Tired of hiding in my room alone with my books. Tired of obsessing about what people think about me. I'm ready for a new start. Ready to open my heart, take risks, give my heart.*

I prayed silently, begging God to make me new, make me brave, make a way for me to find some new friends.

Within a few weeks of arriving at our new house in New Jersey, I'd met several people who would become lifelong best friends. It felt like God stepped in to confirm my decision: I had decided to be different, and he met me there, providing me the opportunities I needed.

But even so, those friendships didn't just fall into my lap—those people didn't walk up to me wearing T-shirts that said, "Talk to me! God sent me to be your future best friend!" I had to put my books and insecurity down and put myself out there. I had to swallow hard, speak up, invite people over. I had to ask questions about their lives and choose to care about them. I had to be honest and brave as I shared my own heart.

All of those things required vulnerability. With each step, there was a risk: They might not want to come over. They might not want a new friend—they might already have friends. They might be interested in friendship but not in friendship with *me*.

But the risks paid off in great rewards: friendships I treasure to this day.

FRIENDSHIP BLOCKERS

So what are some of the feelings and issues that can get in the way of friendship? Let's talk through a few of them.

Insecurity

I'm not as cool [or interesting or athletic or godly or funny or insert whatever trait you're insecure about here] as she is. Why would she want to be my friend? As soon as someone better comes along, she'll start hanging out with them instead. We tend to be hypercritical of ourselves, fixated on our own weaknesses and flaws (flaws that might not even exist!), while other people rarely view us through that same harsh lens. As my dad used to tell me, "Nobody's thinking bad things about you, Elizabeth—they're too busy wondering if you're thinking bad things about them."

Gossip

"Did you hear . . . ?" "Did you know . . . ?" "I'm not supposed to tell anyone this, but . . ." Gossip blocks friendships in multiple ways. Of course it hurts the person we're talking about. But what we don't realize is that it also poisons our friendship with the people who are gossiping with us. It taints our relationship with unkindness, pettiness, and pride.

Conformity

If I'm me, nobody will like me. I just need to blend in, wear the same clothes, pretend to like the same music, talk the same way everyone else does. That's how I'll find friends. When we conform like this, we lose ourselves. We end up paired with people who don't really know us, so we still feel lonely. We may even compromise our convictions for the sake of their approval.

Inaction

Shouldn't friendships just happen naturally? I don't remember having to go look for friends when I was little—they just showed up in my life. I guess I just have to wait and hope the right friend comes along. In my experience, friendship rarely just happens. Potential friends are all around us, but we have to take steps to get to know new people and build new relationships. We might have to be brave and initiate hanging out. We might have to open up and take the conversation a little deeper. Those risks are scary, and they don't pay off in the form of a new bestie every time, but sometimes they do—and that makes the risks worthwhile!

Jealousy

Why is her life so perfect? She's so much prettier/funnier/kinder/more spiritual/more popular than I am. It's not fair. Ugh, I don't think I even want to be friends with someone like that. Jealousy is like insecurity's evil cousin. Insecurity gets the "negative feelings party" started, and jealousy takes it somewhere worse. First, insecurity gets us down on ourselves. Then, if we're not careful, insecurity can twist into resentment, aka jealousy . . . and it's tough to become friends with someone you resent.

Whenever I find one of these blockers in my life, first I pray about it, then I work on making some changes. Awareness first;

action next. To give you a sense of how that works, let's workshop jealousy a bit more. Jealousy was one of the blockers that hounded me throughout my teen years. Insecurity made me feel constantly "less than," and feeling "less than" led to envy and competitiveness, which led to guilt and self-loathing. Woohoo, talk about a super fun cycle! It often started with thoughts like this: *Why is she so pretty when I'm so plain? Why is running so easy for her while I have to torture my lungs just to finish the race? Why does everyone like her, and I feel like a loser?*

As you can imagine, those feelings didn't exactly promote friendship with others! I had to change—I *wanted* to change.

My mom gave me advice that transformed my thinking—and my relationships. She said, "Honey, when you feel jealous of someone, one of two things is going on: either you're jealous of something she has that you can never have and you need to let it go, or you're jealous of something she has that you *could* have, and instead of feeling jealous, you should choose to be inspired and learn from her."

From then on, whenever jealousy reared its hideous green head, I tried to ask myself, *Is this something I can't have and need to let go of, or is it an opportunity to grow?* For example, if I felt jealous of someone I thought was prettier than I was, I needed to let that go. God gave my friend her looks, and he gave me mine. I needed to make peace with my appearance, stop comparing myself to others, and be happy for my friend—and happy with the way God made me.

But what if I was jealous because a friend had gotten a better grade on a test? Well, maybe she had studied hard while I procrastinated—and instead of being jealous of her, I needed to imitate her work ethic.

As I began to work on my thinking in this area, I realized a simple but powerful truth: there's room for everyone on this planet. If God gives someone else success (or something else you want), it doesn't change his plan for your life. Other people don't get *your* blessings. It's not like God sits up in heaven watching you and thinking, *I like So-and-So better, so I'm giving this thing to So-and-So instead.* No—if God gives something to someone, it's because that's his plan for that person. God has a plan for her— and a plan for you! When we accept this, we're less likely to feel jealous of others.

There's room for other people to shine where God wants them to shine and room for you to shine where he wants you to shine! We can celebrate others' victories and successes without worrying that we are somehow missing out.

FRIENDSHIP BOOSTERS

You may not be able to force a new candidate for Favorites in your phone to show up the moment you need one, but that doesn't mean you're completely powerless.

We don't just have to sit around waiting for a friend to fall from the sky. We can all do things that make space for new friends and put us in a better position to connect with people. So what are some friendship boosters that will get you ready to be a great friend? What can make you more available for new relationships?

Pray.

My third grader's dark eyes are pink-rimmed with tears. "Mommy, I don't have any friends in my new class. All my good friends from last year got put in other classes."

My heart gives a twist of sympathy. "I'm sorry, Cassidy. But I bet you'll make some new friends in this class!"

She sniffles. "I don't know. I'll try."

And try she does—for months. But the friendships aren't really clicking, and her little heart stays lonely. Every day she slouches off the school bus sad. I try every Mom trick I can think of to help her make friends, but nothing is working. Finally, one afternoon, we sit on the couch side by side and beg God for help: "God, we know that you see Cassidy's tears and you care about her loneliness. She needs a friend, Father. Please, please, help her find one. Either open up a friendship with someone she already knows or bring someone new into her life. We need you, God. We don't know what to do, but we trust that you hear us."

Several weeks later, I get a message from a family that's thinking about moving to our town and joining our church. "Can you meet us for lunch when we come into town for the job interview?" the mom writes. "It's just an interview, so it may be a while before we get an answer. By the way, we have a daughter, Kayli, who is in third grade."

When we show up for lunch a few days later, the family's eyes are round with shock. They stammer the news: "We just came from the interview, and we got offered the job! They want us to start next week! We need to find a house *tomorrow!*"

A few weeks later, that family moves into a house a few streets away from ours. Kayli is registered to attend Cassidy's school, and Cassidy promises to meet her on the playground at recess. We are amazed—look what God has done! But God has an even bigger surprise in store.

On Kayli's first morning at school, Cassidy looks up after the morning announcements to see Kayli and her mom standing in the doorway of her classroom. Kayli has been assigned to Cassidy's class! Cassidy's little heart almost explodes with joy.

It's been five years, and Kayli and her family have since moved away again (insert lots of sobbing here), but Kayli and Cassidy remain long-distance friends to this day. We still joke with Kayli's family that we prayed them into our lives! To be fair, there have been other lonely times when we have asked God to help us find new friends, and the answer hasn't come as quickly or obviously. But Cassidy and Kayli's friendship reminds me that God truly cares about our relationships. We can take our friendship worries, fears, and desires to him, confident that he cares about our happiness and that even when we can't see it, he's working.

Take risks.

Want to hear a profound truth about friendships? You can't make friends if you don't go make them.

Sounds super simple and obvious, right? But it can be intimidating to put yourself out there—to sit beside someone new in the cafeteria, to ask for someone's number, to invite them to hang out. Sometimes the risks don't pay off—you put yourself out there and the person (who may be insecure themselves) doesn't respond.

But then there are the risks that *do* pay off. Who knows—the girl you reach out to in the lunchroom may keep you snort-laughing at lunch all year long. The new player on your team may end up being a lifelong friend. But you'll never know until you take that first step!

Be openhearted.

I heft my squirming two-year-old, Sawyer, out of her car seat and squeeze her pudgy toddler thighs through the leg holes in the grocery cart. Her bright eyes scan the parking lot, and she squeals: "My friend!"

I follow her pointing finger, expecting to see one of her preschool buddies. But nope, it's a stranger: a toddler perched on her mother's hip. Now my daughter points at the mother: "Mommy friend!"

Mystified, I smile at my daughter. "We don't know those people, Sweetie."

Sawyer just grins and nods. "*My* friend. *Mommy* friend."

Experience has taught me not to argue with a two-year-old, so I give her my "whatever you say" look in return. "Okay, honey. Friends!" As we walk into the store, I smile at the woman and wave at the toddler. They smile and wave back.

This same scene plays out over and over again for months. Every time we're out, when Sawyer spots a mother and child nearby, she happily—and loudly—pronounces them our friends. And after a while, her message starts to sink in: *Potential friends are everywhere! I just need to notice them.*

I have a feeling that this openheartedness—this easy affection, this willingness to love without the fear of being hurt—is one of the reasons Jesus told us to "become like little children" (Matthew 18:3). Sometimes we tell ourselves we can't make any friends, but the truth is, little Sawyer knew a secret we all need to learn: potential friends are everywhere, if we'll just open our eyes—and our hearts.

Be selfless.

Sometimes we are so focused on wanting to have a friend that we forget about what we have to give. Maybe instead of worrying about finding someone to be *your* friend, you can look around to see if someone else needs you to be *their* friend. As Jesus said,

> Give, and it will be given to you. A good measure, pressed down, shaken together and running over, will be poured into your lap. For with the measure you use, it will be measured to you.
>
> LUKE 6:38

The more you give to others, the more you'll receive. If you're stingy with your heart, chances are others will be stingy with theirs too. But if you're generous with your heart, others are more likely to be generous with theirs. If you give away kindness and thoughtfulness, you are far more likely to receive the same in return.

This isn't a money-back guarantee. Every time you're kind to someone, they may not be kind in return; every time you initiate a friendship, you may not get a great response. But it's a principle that generally holds true. Start giving your friendship away, and watch what happens.

Be the friend you wish you had.

Jesus encouraged us, "Do to others what you would have them do to you" (Matthew 7:12). Following Jesus' wisdom can transform your friendships. What do you wish your friends (or potential friends) would do for you? Now go out and do those things for them!

Many times we stay stuck at the "introductory level" of friendship because no one is brave enough to go deeper. Because we feel insecure, we wait for the other person to initiate: *I wish she'd text me. I wish she'd ask me to sit with her at the game. I wish she'd invite me to go to the movies.* But if we will take a risk and do what we wish someone would do for us, we open up opportunities for a deeper relationship.

Other times we get stuck in friendship because we make it all about us—what we can get. *I wish someone would be there for me. I wish someone cared about my life.* And if we start keeping score in our friendships—*I called her last time; now it's her turn to call me*—well, that's when things get unhealthy. We're much happier in our friendships when we focus on what we can give instead of what a friend is giving to us.

So . . . what do you wish your friends would do for you?

- Do you wish they'd check on you when they know you're stressed?

- Do you wish they'd text you an "I'm praying for you" before a big test?
- Do you wish they'd go out of their way to include you in group conversations?
- Do you wish they'd stand up for you when a group text goes from sarcastic to mean?
- Do you wish they'd forgive you and give you a second chance when you need it?

Well . . . do those things for others! Be the friend you wish you had. Many people will respond to your kindness with kindness in return.

Remember where your confidence comes from.

The Bible tells us that our confidence shouldn't come from people. Instead, it should come from God:

> It is better to take refuge in the LORD
> than to trust in humans.
>
> PSALM 118:8

People change; God never does. People sin; God never does. God is the friend who will always be there and never let us down.

* * *

It's a priceless gift to have friends who are Christians—friends who share your love for God and your desire to honor him, people who understand your priorities and encourage your faith. What a blessing it is to be able to honestly share your struggles, pray through hard times and tough choices, and help each other grow in Christ. And friends like this don't come along every day.

"Friendship chemistry"—even with other believers—can be

Quiz: The Friendship Checkup

So let's say you have a friendship, but you're starting to feel like something's off. How can you tell if a friendship is a relationship to keep investing in? Take the quiz, give yourself points based on the scoring chart below, and then add up your total.

	THE FRIENDSHIP CHECKUP	Rarely	Sometimes	Often
1.	Do I enjoy being with this friend?			
2.	Can I be myself with this person?			
3.	Do I like the person I am when I hang out with this friend?			
4.	Does being with this person make me more godly?			
5.	If I feel uncomfortable about something, can I talk to my friend about it?			
6.	Does this friend respect me and my convictions?			
7.	Does this friend listen to me?			
8.	Does this person apologize when they've hurt my feelings?			
9.	Does this person forgive me when I've hurt them?			
10.	Is this person trustworthy?			
	SUBTOTAL			
	TOTAL			

SCORING
Rarely = 1
Sometimes = 2
Often = 3

KEY
24–30 = Looking good! Keep building into that friendship.
18–23 = It's tune-up time. Try adding more of God—and yourself—into this friendship.
Less than 18 = You've got some thinking and praying to do. Maybe it's time to seek advice from a parent or spiritual mentor to discuss how this relationship is going.

challenging, even frustrating. It can be tough to find someone who is like minded *and* "like hearted"—someone who not only clicks with your personality and shares your interests but also shares your heart for God. I've talked to many girls who struggle to connect with the girls in their church, and that can be discouraging. If you've struggled to connect, and you sometimes feel lonely even in your youth group, know that you aren't the only one. Keep taking the steps we've talked about—prayer, selflessness, open-heartedness. Try to give your heart to the people who are currently in your life, and rely on God to support you as you wait and pray for deeper, closer connections. God sees your heart and knows your needs.

As much as we need and enjoy friendships with other believers, it's great to have friends who aren't Christians too. Jesus calls us to share his message of grace with the world, and we can't do that if we don't go out into the world and get to know people from all different backgrounds. Jesus was known as a man who had meaningful relationships with all kinds of people—he was even called the friend of sinners (see Matthew 11:19). Over time, Jesus helped many of those people to find faith and salvation. Like Jesus, let's offer our friendship to others, praying that God allows us to be an influence for him as we go.

FRIENDSHIP WITH GOD

No matter how your friendships are going right now, keep this in mind: you already have the best friend anyone could imagine. He will never be too busy or distracted or caught up in his own life when you need to talk. He will always pick up when you call, and he'll never cut your stories short. He will never forget your birthday, never get in a bad mood, never shut you down. He will never change, never leave, never fail. He will always listen, always forgive, always love. The Bible puts it this way:

The LORD himself goes before you and will be with you;
he will never leave you nor forsake you. Do not be afraid;
do not be discouraged.

DEUTERONOMY 31:8

Now that's a friendship to count on. That's a best friend forever.

FEELING YOUR WAY FORWARD

Journal Prompts

1. Which friendship blocker do you struggle with most often?
2. Which friendship booster would you like to begin working on?
3. Describe the kind of friend you'd like to find.
4. Describe the kind of friend you'd like to be.
5. How do you feel about your friendships? If you could change one thing about your friendships, what would it be?

Prayer Prompt

Let your unfailing love surround us, LORD,
   for our hope is in you alone.

PSALM 33:22, NLT

Lifelines

Five Scriptures about friendship:

1. Proverbs 13:20
2. Luke 17:3-4
3. Proverbs 17:17
4. Proverbs 27:4
5. Philippians 2:3-4

CHAPTER 10

PRAYING THROUGH ALL YOUR EMOTIONS

I'm sitting in my quiet-time spot—the comfy chair in the corner between two windows. I'm reading, praying, thinking. The world outside my windows is hushed but alert, night's velvet black giving way to barely-there gray.

I am praying my way through Psalm 139 for the ten thousandth time: "You have searched me, LORD, and you know me. You know when I sit and when I rise; you perceive my thoughts from afar. You discern my going out and my lying down; you are familiar with all my ways. Before a word is on my tongue you, LORD, know it completely. . . ."

God, thank you for taking the time to get to know me so well. You could spend all your energy just keeping the universe running, but you make time for me. Thank you for wanting *to know what's going on in my life and in my heart.*

Outside, fog creeps across the ground, tickling the grass. *Wake up. The sun is coming.*

I read on: "For you created my inmost being; you knit me together in my mother's womb. I praise you because I am"—my breath catches—"fearfully and wonderfully made." I've read these words before, but now I stop. I think.

God created my inmost being. The real me. The inner me. Complicated me—quick with my tears and fierce in my love.

For as long as I can remember, I've longed to have someone to understand me—how I can hope so hard it hurts, how my heart sprouts wings every time I walk under springtime cherry trees, how a good book can sweep me away, how guilty feelings so often nag me. I have always wanted someone to love me, all of me, for who I am—all my colorful tangle of big feelings and dreams. I have always wanted someone to share life with me: to care about my family, my school stress, my friendships, my doubts, my insecurities. To laugh with me, cry with me, *be there* with me.

I read on: "Where can I flee from your presence? If I go up to the heavens, you are there; if I make my bed in the depths, you are there."

And it hits me: *I already have the relationship I've been longing for.* I already have someone who understands me even better than I understand myself. I already have someone who appreciates my silly quirks and cheesy sense of humor. I already have someone who wants to hear all my angsty stories. I already have someone who patiently listens as I talk through my doubts and guilty feelings for the millionty billionth time.

I have God.

And whether you realize it or not, you have him too.

God longs to be close to you. Not just "Long-Distance Grandparent Who Sends You Presents on Holidays" close, not just "Friend You Talk to between Classes" close, not just "Youth Leader You Meet with for Advice" close. No, God wants to share daily life with you. All day, every day, for the rest of your life. He isn't separated by distance or limited by time. He's always available, always interested. He's never too busy, never overbooked, never out of town. He's never in a bad mood, never selfish, never distracted, never too tired to listen.

The Creator of the universe, the Beginning and the End, the Light of the world, the Life Giver and Star Spinner—he cares about you. And he cares about what you care about. If something makes you sad, he wants to know. If something makes you happy, he wants to celebrate with you. If something makes you anxious, nervous, giddy, flustered, insecure, or embarrassed, he cares. If it matters to you, it matters to him.

Isn't! That! Amazing?

A DIVINE INVITATION

Sometimes the prayers we hear in church can sound formal and intimidating. They use lots of flowery words and "holy" language. They sound more like a Shakespearean play than words a regular person would speak to a close friend.

Of course it's fine if people enjoy praying that way, but it's certainly not the *only* way to pray (or even the best way). If that's not your style, you don't have to pray like that. Prayer is simply a conversation between you and God. It's an opportunity for you to share what's on your mind and heart. A chance to ask him for help, thank him for blessings, and talk through life.

When I was in high school, my bedroom overlooked our grassy backyard, and if I glanced out of my window early in the morning, I might see my dad disappearing into the trees behind our house, off for his morning prayer walk in the woods. I always watched with mingled awe and guilt, longing to feel as close to God and as excited about prayer as Dad did.

Over the years I've worked to nurture my own walk with God. It's different from my dad's, but it's special, it's meaningful, and it's mine. I encourage you to develop your own habit of talking with God—one that helps you connect with your Father in heaven.

The Bible is how God shares his heart with us; prayer is how we share our hearts with God. God is so excited about hearing from us, so eager to help us learn how to speak to him, that he put an entire book of prayers in the Bible: the Psalms.

This book contains 150 different prayers and songs. In those psalms, we find people bringing every imaginable feeling to God: joy, gratitude, depression, loneliness, discouragement, hopefulness, anger, bitterness, fear, worry, regret, envy, insecurity, embarrassment, excitement, joy . . . the list could go on and on.

As you can see, some of those feelings are positive emotions we enjoy, while others are ones we wish we could avoid; some are righteous, and others are not. But God put them in Scripture to show us that he's willing to listen to *all* of them!

That means you can pray . . .

- when you're in a bad mood;
- when you aren't in a great place spiritually;
- when you're feeling angry or confused or rebellious;
- when you're anxious or depressed.

Now, prayer isn't just a place for venting—spewing your unfiltered emotions—although you will find plenty of examples of people venting to God in the psalms. Prayer is the place where we express our feelings and then *work through them* with God. Just as we talk to friends or family when we need to sort through feelings, and they help us find resolution and solutions, we can talk to God and ask him to help us process and move forward.

And the great news? God is always there, no matter how we feel. We may have off days (or weeks or months!) in our prayer life, but God never does. We may have off days (or weeks or months!) in our walk of faith—times when we aren't as faithful or righteous as we want to be—but God loves us through our growing pains and mistakes. And he always will. God wants to talk to you, no matter what.

PRAYER IS BIGGER THAN YOUR FEELINGS

For many years, I searched for feelings in my relationship with God—emotional *zings* that confirmed, "Yes! I'm close to God, and he's close to me!" I would hear other Christians talk about how they cried during their prayers or felt excited or had all kinds of warm fuzzies, and I didn't have those feelings all that often. I described one of my more emotional prayers at the beginning of this chapter, but honestly, I don't have experiences like that very often.

My prayers were honest, but mostly they were kind of matter of fact. Even though I was a big feeler, I didn't have a lot of crying and warm-fuzzying going on in my prayers from day to day. So I always felt vaguely guilty, wondering if my prayer life was inferior to others', kind of boring—maybe even insincere. I wondered if maybe I wasn't doing it right.

But you know what? Prayer isn't a feeling. Prayer works sort of like our close friendships. Some days you feel all the friends-forever feels, and other days, you're just like, "Hey, how's it going? Cool. We're all good." In your relationship with God, you'll have some days when you feel inspired or moved or grateful; other days you'll just show up and talk to God about what's on your mind without fireworks or epic background music.

If you're a steady or reluctant feeler, you may be breathing a sigh of relief: *Thank goodness it's not all about feelings!* And if you're a big feeler, you might be glad to know that while God welcomes your big feelings, they don't set the tone of the relationship. Even when your feelings fluctuate, they don't change your relationship. God stays the same no matter how you're feeling from day to day (or minute to minute!).

Our closeness with God doesn't depend on how we feel—it depends on God's love. And while our feelings change all the time, God's love never does.

WAYS TO PRAY

Have you ever had a friendship get stuck? You like each other, but you can't ever think of new things to do, so you end up doing the same thing over and over again. After a while, you get bored in the relationship because it's in a rut. It's not fun, not growing, not taking either one of you anywhere new. Sometimes we get stuck in a rut in our prayer lives too. Maybe you only pray for a few minutes before bed, or you only pray when you're in a panic over a crisis in your life, or you only pray first thing in the morning before school. We've all been there, and before long we may begin to feel bored and stale in our walk with God.

If your prayer life needs some spicing up, here are some ideas to try:

- Go for a prayer walk. Walk around outside and talk to God as you walk. When I do this, I always find that I end up feeling more grateful and inspired. I'm more aware of God's creation and power and less focused on my problems.
- Sit outside and pray. Take a little time to thank God for the world he created.
- Listen to your favorite worship songs as a way of praying. You can either sing them to God or tell him what the words mean to you.
- Find a psalm that expresses whatever you're feeling that day. Read one verse to God, tell him what that verse means to you, and then move on to the next verse.
- Write a song or psalm of your own to God.

- Pray a "thanksgiving only" prayer. Devote a prayer time specifically to thanking God—no "asks" allowed! I find it especially helpful to thank God like this when I'm feeling discouraged—it reminds me how much I have to be thankful for.
- Keep a prayer journal. Write down your prayers like letters to God. This is how I pray most days. It helps me focus on what I'm saying to God and keeps my thoughts from wandering.
- Keep a prayer list for friends, family, and yourself, and pray your way through the list regularly. You'll be amazed to see how many of your prayers God specifically answers over time.
- Before you go to bed at night, write down any prayers that God answered that day—even if they were small prayers like, "Please, God, let me find someone to sit with at lunch!" Take a moment to thank God for those kindnesses.
- Write down a list of "impossible prayers"—things you dream about God doing even though they seem impossible. Start praying for those things every day, and watch what God does!
- Use the Lord's Prayer as an outline. Take each line as a prompt for a different topic in your prayer. For example, the Lord's Prayer begins with the words "Our Father in heaven." You could begin your prayer by thanking God for being your Father and for the ways he has taken care of you lately. Continue to pray through the rest of the prayer, line by line, topic by topic.

WAYS TO RELATE TO GOD

Scripture uses several different analogies to help us understand how to relate to God. Each description helps us feel closer to God in different ways and gives us ideas for how to connect with him:

God is our Father.

> The LORD your God, who is going before you, will
> fight for you, as he did for you in Egypt, before your
> very eyes, and in the wilderness. There you saw how
> the LORD your God carried you, as a father carries his son,
> all the way you went until you reached this place.
>
> DEUTERONOMY 1:30-31

If you don't have a close relationship with your human father, either because he isn't in your life or because the relationship is difficult, God wants to be the Dad you wish you had. He is a doting father who thinks you are the best kid in the world. He is proud of you. He wants to protect you. If anyone messes with you, his "How Dare You Mess with My Girl" rage flares. When you need something, it gives him joy to provide it. When you're happy or excited, his eyes light up to match yours. He wants the best for you.

God is a Friend.

> The LORD is a friend to those who fear him.
> He teaches them his covenant.
>
> PSALM 25:14, NLT

My friend Emma and I love to be together. We could sit for hours and never run out of stories, deep thoughts, memories, and jokes. In a single afternoon we may go from laughing to crying to confessing to reminiscing, then back to laughing again. And sometimes we sip tea in silence, just happy to be in the same room. I always want to spend time with Emma. Just being near her makes me happy. I want to know what she thinks about everything. I want her advice on my decisions. When good things happen, I call her; when terrible things happen, I call her.

Wouldn't it be great to feel that way about God? Excited to be with him, happy and comfortable in his presence, fascinated by his stories and ideas? Basking in the simple pleasure of spending time with someone we love—who loves us in return?

Friendship with God is different from human friendship, of course. We aren't peers with God, and there's always a level of respect we maintain for his authority and power. And yet we can bring some elements of friendship into our relationship with God. We can share the small details and worries of life with him, confident that he cares; we can cry with him, depend on him, seek advice from him, even laugh with him.

When I have big feelings, I love sharing the moment with God—especially if it's something I might be embarrassed to share with people. Maybe it's how my heart did a happy dance when I saw a rainbow or how the sound of rain made me want to curl up in a cozy-under-the-covers way or how I spit on myself when I met a new person and then I felt like a royal idiot or how I'm just deep-down-in-my-bones tired and I wish life were easier.

No human friend can be present for every little feeling we long to share—but God can. If something's on your mind or heart, take it to him—he wants to share it with you.

As with any relationship, the more time, energy, and heart you invest, the more joy, connection, and fulfillment you'll experience.

God is our Protector.

God is our refuge and strength,
    an ever-present help in trouble.
Therefore we will not fear, though the earth give way
    and the mountains fall into the heart of the sea,
though its waters roar and foam
    and the mountains quake with their surging.

PSALM 46:1-3

God is also the one who steps in to protect us—he is our refuge and place of safety. Even when waters roar and mountains fall in your life—when a friendship crumbles or sickness strikes or a family fights. God is our safe house, our place of refuge. The thing about places of refuge, though, is they do us no good if we don't go to them when a storm comes. A tornado shelter can't keep us safe if we're standing outside just watching the storm!

I recently had a high-pressure week, and I didn't make time to be with God the way I needed to—I let my busy schedule sweep me away. All week I felt stressed out, anxious, and a bit distant from God. I didn't feel his comfort. But does that mean God wasn't available, wasn't ready and eager to help me? Nope—it means I didn't seek his help, didn't go to him. The safe place was waiting, the door unlocked and open, but I never showed up.

If mountains are quaking and waters are roaring in your life, I encourage you to go to God as your protector. Open God's Word and let him speak to you; let his wisdom help you sift through your fears and feelings. Then speak back to him in prayer, inviting him in to help and to heal. That's when you will experience God as ever present, ever helpful, ever strong. That's how God will become your refuge and strength, your protector.

He's there even now, ready to help, doors wide open, waiting for you to walk in, sit down, and take shelter from the storm.

WORKING OUT INTENSE FEELINGS WITH GOD

God has blessed me with some patient people who listen to my angsty feelings and help me work through them, and believe me, I have poured out my junk in many a tear-filled, hand-wringing, tissue-twisting conversation. But the trouble is, even when people help me work through a feeling, some residue remains. We may be done talking, but I'm not done feeling. I'm still twitchy—or worse. I learned long ago that I have to finish my feelings with

God. People can't do for me what only God and the Spirit were meant to do.

- People can't give us peace—God gives us peace.
- People can't ease our conscience—only God can do that.
- People can't give us a change of heart—God changes hearts.
- People can't forgive us when we sin against God—God forgives.

Here's what I do when I have a feeling (or feelings) I can't get rid of. First, I spend some time alone with God. I tell him what's on my mind. I try to describe the feeling as specifically as I can. I usually have to write it down to really get it out properly. When I have lots of big, tangled feelings, if I try talking or praying in my head I usually end up all over the place, rambling with no end in sight: "I feel angry because so-and-so was unfair and it brought up a million insecurities and doesn't she know that's unkind and hurts people and how could she act like that and I know Jesus doesn't want us to judge, but seriously, why do people act like that and I feel guilty because I kind of want you to punish her and that's sinful and now I feel like a horrible person and I'm sorry and I know I need grace too and you won't forgive me unless I forgive her and—" You see what I mean? Not very productive. It's not that God isn't patient enough to listen to our rambles, but when I wander around like this, I end up frustrating myself! I don't feel resolved when I'm done praying.

It helps if I start by writing down what I'm feeling. I simplify and streamline it as much as possible:

- What happened?
- How did it make me feel?
- What did it make me think?

- What insecurity/sin/bad memory did it bring up?
- What do I want God to do about this situation?
- What does God want me to do about this situation (if anything)?
- What would help me let go of this feeling?

Then I pray my way through this list. I like to write down my prayer, just like a letter. By the end of my prayer, I try to reach a resolution. This is the tricky part. I tell God,

Here's what I am asking you to do about this feeling [or situation, relationship, or worry]. Here's what I think you want me to do. I'm presenting my decision and plan to you, asking you to guide me somewhere else if I'm not on the right path. Now I ask you to enable me to follow through, and I leave this [worry/fear/insecurity/ problem/situation/person] with you, in your capable hands. I trust that you are aware and engaged and in control. I give this to you, God. I trust you. Please help me to feel differently soon—to feel more [peace or forgiveness or whatever it is I need to feel]. I know I may not feel different right away, but please move me toward the right feeling. In the meantime, I choose to focus on something else while you work. I choose to act like I feel better, trusting that you can help my feelings to follow my actions.

I still sometimes end my prayers feeling a bit funky, but I'm usually calmer, more focused, and more aware of what God thinks and what he wants me to do moving forward.

* * *

I'm nineteen, and I'm home from college for the summer. One night, I overhear Dad telling Mom that he's going running early the next morning—like, way earlier than any nineteen-year-old wants to wake up. Dad and I used to run together sometimes, and theoretically I'd like to go, but . . . yikes, that's *early*. I keep my mouth shut, not wanting to make a promise my exhausted body can't keep. But come morning, the gray light of a waking sun peeks through my windows and nudges me awake. And I remember: *running with Dad*.

Rubbing sleep from my eyes, I stumble out of bed and into my running clothes. I slip into the dark hallway, nearly colliding with Dad at the top of the stairs. Even in the darkness, I can see his eyes light up with joy.

"Oh! You're coming!" He wraps me in a hug, and in the squeeze of his strong arms, I hear his words, feel his love: *I'm so happy just to be with you. So happy you want to be with me.*

God wants to be with you, to spend time with you. He loves to hear your thoughts, carry your feelings, know your heart. He wants to hear your worries, your fears, your joys—and all the mess and madness between.

God is waiting with wide-open arms to draw closer to you. He's eager to comfort your hurts, cheer your victories, calm your storms, and simply share your life—and all its feelings. So go ahead—talk to him. He's listening.

FEELING YOUR WAY FORWARD

Journal Prompts

1. How do you find it easiest to relate to God: as your Father, your friend, or your protector? Why do you think you connect best with him in that way?

2. When do you feel the most emotionally connected to God?
3. Which of the prayer strategies listed on pages 134–135 would you like to try out?

Prayer Prompt

As the deer pants for streams of water,
    so my soul pants for you, my God.
My soul thirsts for God, for the living God.
    When can I go and meet with God?

PSALM 42:1-2

Lifelines

Five Scriptures about prayer and relating to God:

1. Luke 18:1-8
2. Proverbs 10:25
3. 1 Thessalonians 5:16-18
4. James 5:16
5. Matthew 6:9-13

CHAPTER 11

WHEN GUILT COMES KNOCKING

When I was sixteen, my dad tried teaching me how to play tennis. He thought we'd have fun. (Wrong.) He thought I'd be good. (*So* wrong.)

It went something like this:

Dad lobs an easy serve over the net. I swing—*whoosh*—so hard I spin in a complete circle.

"Sorry!" I call, feeling heat starting in my face as I chase the ball.

Dad sends over another baby serve. I make contact, but the ball goes wild—like, over-the-fence-and-into-the-parking-lot wild.

"Sorry!" I call again, my cheeks on fire.

Twenty more serves, twenty more wild swings, twenty more rounds of "I'm sorry."

Dad finally gets frustrated—but not at my horrific tennis playing. "Honey, would you please stop apologizing? You're making me feel like a mean coach or something! Stop saying you're sorry!"

I nod vigorously. "Right. Sure. Sorry."

Dad (slapping a hand over his eyes): "Argh!"

Welcome to my guilty world.

*   *   *

If I had to describe how I usually felt in high school using only one word, the word would be—you guessed it—*guilty*. My prayer life was one apology after another. *I'm sorry, God. So sorry. I'm not good enough. Not devoted enough. Not perfect enough. Not pure enough. Not wholehearted enough.*

I was wearing myself out. If Christianity were a long swim toward heaven, I was swimming in a suit of armor, and I was drowning.

If you always feel guilty or if you often suspect that God is angry with you or if you never feel like you're good enough, this chapter is for you. God doesn't want his beloved daughters tiptoe-ing around him, terrified of his anger, insecure in their salvation, unsure of his love. Even if they're terrible tennis players.

YOU HAVE A DEFENDER

Did you know that one of the reasons Jesus came to earth was so he could understand how hard it is for us to deal with tempta-tion? Jesus stands at the Father's right hand and asks him to give us grace, saying, "I know firsthand how hard this is. She needs a lot of grace." The Bible describes it like this:

> We do not have a high priest who is unable to empathize
> with our weaknesses, but we have one who has been
> tempted in every way, just as we are—yet he did not
> sin. Let us then approach God's throne of grace with
> confidence, so that we may receive mercy and find grace
> to help us in our time of need.
>
> HEBREWS 4:14-16

Thanks to Jesus, we can approach the throne of grace with confidence. Notice it's not the throne of power (though God is all-powerful) or the throne of fear (though God is fearsome). It's the throne of *grace*.

GODLY SORROW VERSUS WORLDLY SORROW

You may be thinking, *But I still feel guilty! I'm pretty sure I sinned! What do I do when I mess up?* There are times when we are plagued by false guilt or exaggerated guilt (aka feeling horrible over missing-a-tennis-ball-type stuff). But other times we have sinned against God and others, and the guilt we feel is a sign of the Holy Spirit's conviction. So how can we tell the difference?

Here's a Scripture that helps me when I sin—or think I've sinned—and I need help sorting it out:

> The kind of sorrow God wants us to experience leads us away from sin and results in salvation. There's no regret for that kind of sorrow. But worldly sorrow, which lacks repentance, results in spiritual death.
>
> Just see what this godly sorrow produced in you! Such earnestness, such concern to clear yourselves, such indignation, such alarm, such longing to see me, such zeal, and such a readiness to punish wrong. You showed that you have done everything necessary to make things right.
>
> 2 CORINTHIANS 7:10-11, NLT

When we sin (and we *all* sin plenty of times, even as Christians), there's a proper response: it's called godly sorrow. But there's another kind of guilty feeling—a harmful one that's not from God. This is called worldly sorrow. Let's take a look at the difference between the two:

GODLY SORROW	WORLDLY SORROW
Intended by God	Not intended by God
Hurts temporarily	Lasts too long
Brings repentance	Unproductive
Leaves no regret	Harmful
Leads to salvation	Brings death

Godly sorrow doesn't mean sitting around hating yourself, telling yourself how horrible you are and how you don't deserve to go to heaven (aka wallowing or lying in a puddle of I'm-an-awful-person mush on the floor). Godly sorrow prompts us to feel emotions that lead us to actions. Godly sorrow may sound (and feel) something like this:

Earnestness: *I'm not going to stretch the truth, sidestep responsibility, or avoid dealing with this.*

Indignation: *This is wrong. It violates God's ways, and I need to stop.*

Concern to clear yourself: *Have I hurt anyone? How can I set things right with God and with people?*

Alarm: *Whoa! I can't ignore this.*

These emotions push us to take action, to change. The Bible calls this "repentance." Repentance means you change your mind—and change your direction. Repentance isn't just sitting around feeling bad; repentance bears the fruit of change in our lives. As John the Baptist said, "Produce fruit in keeping with repentance" (Luke 3:8).

When we identify sin, feel godly sorrow, and choose to repent, God is waiting to wrap his arms around us. (Take a look at the parable of the Prodigal Son in Luke 15—the son begins his apology speech, but his father is so thrilled to have him back that he doesn't even let him finish!)

Here are some specific biblical actions we might take when we repent:

- Turn to God with your sin (see Acts 3:19-20).
- Confess to a trusted friend, seeking prayer and healing (see James 5:16).
- Cut off sin, even if it means taking radical steps (see Matthew 5:27-30).
- If you have sinned against another person, set things right as you are able (see Luke 19:8-10).
- Seek forgiveness in prayer (see Luke 11:4).

If your guilty feelings are pointing you toward one of these actions, you'll probably find that once you follow through, the guilty feelings begin to fade, gradually replaced by a sense of joy and freedom.

FINDING RESOLUTION WITH GOD

Have you ever gotten in an argument with a friend but you weren't willing—or able—to apologize, so things stayed weird between you? Until you have the conversation where you say, "Hey, I messed up, and I'm sorry. Will you forgive me so we can start over?" you're probably going to feel insecure and unresolved.

In the same way, when we do something that hurts God, we find healing by acknowledging our mistakes, apologizing, and making changes. It's not that an apology earns God's forgiveness, but it does clear the air. Apology is more for our benefit than for God's. It helps our hearts when we speak the words, "I'm sorry. Please forgive me." God is always ready to forgive and restore the relationship.

If you're a reluctant feeler, you might prefer to avoid dealing

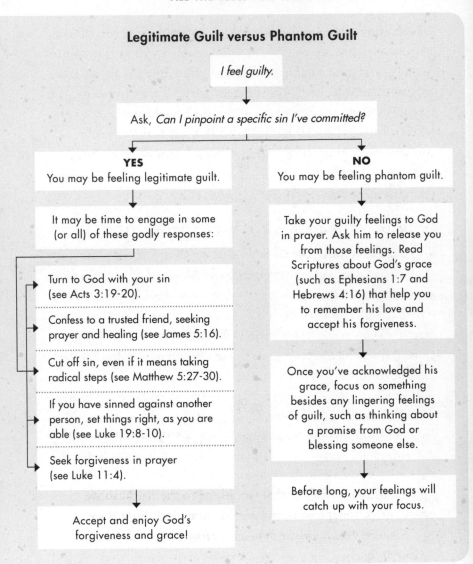

Legitimate Guilt versus Phantom Guilt

I feel guilty.

Ask, *Can I pinpoint a specific sin I've committed?*

YES
You may be feeling legitimate guilt.

It may be time to engage in some (or all) of these godly responses:

Turn to God with your sin (see Acts 3:19-20).

Confess to a trusted friend, seeking prayer and healing (see James 5:16).

Cut off sin, even if it means taking radical steps (see Matthew 5:27-30).

If you have sinned against another person, set things right, as you are able (see Luke 19:8-10).

Seek forgiveness in prayer (see Luke 11:4).

Accept and enjoy God's forgiveness and grace!

NO
You may be feeling phantom guilt.

Take your guilty feelings to God in prayer. Ask him to release you from those feelings. Read Scriptures about God's grace (such as Ephesians 1:7 and Hebrews 4:16) that help you to remember his love and accept his forgiveness.

Once you've acknowledged his grace, focus on something besides any lingering feelings of guilt, such as thinking about a promise from God or blessing someone else.

Before long, your feelings will catch up with your focus.

with guilty feelings when you sin—you'd rather pretend they don't exist and hope they'll go away. But ignoring sin always backfires! The sooner you set things straight, the sooner you'll feel better with God. If you're a steady feeler, don't be afraid to pause and take the time you need to think and pray through guilty feelings when they show up—they may feel like a distraction from more practical things on your agenda, but they deserve time and attention now so they don't pack a bigger punch later. If you're a big feeler, you don't have to be overwhelmed by—or afraid of—guilt when it comes. Understanding the difference between godly sorrow and worldly sorrow can help you distinguish between legitimate guilt and phantom guilt, make changes if you need to, and embrace the grace and joy God has for you.

WORLDLY SORROW AND PHANTOM GUILT

We've talked about how to experience godly sorrow, repent, and apologize when you find sin in your life. But some of us feel guilty all the time, no matter what. We live with worldly sorrow and phantom guilt. Worldly sorrow is when you try to earn your own forgiveness by punishing yourself and living in misery; phantom guilt is when you *feel* guilty, but you're not actually guilty. You feel like you're in sin, but you're not actually in sin.

Misplaced or exaggerated guilty feelings can be a tool Satan uses to torment us. He figures, "I can't trip her up with sin right now, so I'll get her with excessive guilt instead!" The Bible describes the struggle like this:

> Our actions will show that we belong to the truth, so we will be confident when we stand before God. *Even if we feel guilty, God is greater than our feelings, and he knows everything.*
>
> Dear friends, if we don't feel guilty, we can come to God with bold confidence. And we will receive from him whatever we ask because we obey him and do the things that please him.
>
> 1 JOHN 3:19-22, NLT (EMPHASIS ADDED)

Sometimes we feel guilty, but our feelings are wrong. "God is greater than our feelings, and he knows everything"—even the places in our own hearts we don't understand.

So how can we tell the difference between legitimate guilt and phantom guilt? I've learned to ask my guilty feeling a simple question: "What do you want from me?" Phantom guilt won't have any helpful answers; it will just suggest things like, *I want you to slouch around feeling like a worthless slug for the next three months. I want you to lose your confidence and stop using your gifts for God.* Or it might sound something like this: *I'm in sin. I'm not sure exactly what sin, but I know I'm doing something wrong. I'm sure if I think hard enough, I'll think of a dozen Bad Things I've done in the past day or so. I can tell God is mad at me. There's no way I'm making it to heaven. All that grace stuff sounds amazing, but it's not for me—it's only for those people who are perfect.*

It's easy to spot phantom guilt on paper, isn't it? But it's not as easy to identify when it's whispering in your head—it's a very convincing voice!

On the other hand, when you ask legitimate guilt, "What do you want?" it will have practical, purposeful actions in mind—actions like the five things we listed in the sidebar on page 148.

Phantom guilt keeps us feeling condemned even when we've been saved by grace. We've received the gift of salvation, but phantom guilt keeps us from enjoying it. Jesus has won the victory for our souls, but Satan is still claiming victory over our feelings. It's like he's saying, "I may have lost the war, but I can still win a battle—the battle for her joy. I can ruin God's gift for her!"

Oh, the enemy is a nasty one, isn't he? He wants you to feel lost even when you're saved. To feel like God is finger pointing and frowning in disapproval, even when he's overflowing with fatherly pride.

WHAT ABOUT CONSEQUENCES?

My senior year of high school, I crammed into a car with a few friends, all of us decked out in green and white, excited to cheer for our school's basketball team in the division championship. I had my parents' permission to go to the game . . . *however*. When I asked permission, I neglected to mention that the game was a two-hour drive away and I wouldn't get home till after midnight. Yeah. Minor details. The kind of details parents like to know. On the way home, the car broke down (*of course* the car broke down), and my friends and I ended up stranded at a Waffle House in the Middle of Nowhere, North Carolina, until my uncle finally arrived to pick us up. At 1 a.m.

When I got home, my parents and I talked it all out. I apologized (as you might imagine, lots of tears and snot were involved), and my parents forgave me. But my thoughtlessness and pride still had consequences. Two weeks later, when my school played in the state championship game, guess who didn't get to go? Yours truly.

Was I forgiven? Yes.

Were my parents still angry with me two weeks later? No.

But were there still consequences for my dumb decisions? Yes.

Even when we're forgiven by God, we may live with some consequences from our poor choices and past sins. And sometimes we feel condemned by those consequences—they make us wonder if God is still angry with us or hasn't forgiven us after all. But consequences don't mean condemnation.

God can totally love you—and use you to do great things for him—even as you live with lingering reminders of your past mistakes. Think about these examples from Scripture:

- When God gave Moses the miraculous power to bring water from a rock, he specifically instructed Moses to speak to the rock, not strike it. But Moses got carried away and hit the rock with his staff. As a result, he wasn't able to lead the Israelites into the Promised Land. He died before the Israelites entered it. Even so, he continued to lead God's people and was honored in death as a great man of God. God did show Moses some grace by allowing him to see the Promised Land from a distance before he died (see Numbers 20:1-13; Deuteronomy 34).

- Abraham and his wife Sarah longed to have a baby of their own, but Sarah couldn't get pregnant. God had promised them a baby, but years passed and Sarah's arms stayed empty. No baby. After years of waiting, Sarah gave up on God's plan and came up with her own. She urged Abraham to have a child with a concubine (kind of like a second wife). This decision resulted in heartache and conflict in Sarah and Abraham's marriage. But God didn't take back his promise: Sarah later had a baby boy, Isaac (see Genesis 16; 21).

- The apostle Peter, one of Jesus' closest friends, denied the Lord three times on the night Jesus was arrested. Peter lied; he cursed; he cowered. When he realized what he had done—and what was going to happen to Jesus—Peter "went outside and wept bitterly" (Luke 22:62). When Jesus rose from the dead, he and Peter had some things to work through (see John 21:15-23). But they did work it out, and Jesus forgave Peter. In spite of this betrayal, Peter still got to play a powerful role leading the early church in Jerusalem.

Even though Christians are forgiven and free, we may live with some fallout from our past decisions. Maybe you slacked off in school for a while, and even though you are working hard and making better grades now, your GPA is still lower than you want it to be. Maybe you did something that hurt a friend, and even though you've tried to make things right, the relationship isn't the same. Maybe you made some mistakes in a dating relationship that you now regret, and even though you are forgiven by God, made pure by the forgiveness of Christ, sometimes the memories come back to haunt you. But you know what? Even if you are living with consequences, you are no less forgiven, no less loved than any other Christian. (Welcome to the We All Have Sinful Pasts Club. I have my membership card; you have yours.) If you've been washed in the blood of Christ, you can stand confidently in God's grace.

And guess what? Being a Christian doesn't mean you'll never sin or make mistakes. Sometimes our "old self" makes an appearance, and sin creeps in. Other times we make unwise choices, and we have to live with them for a while. Even so, you can stand cleansed and confident in the grace of God, thanks to the blood of Christ.

IN CHRIST

Let's step back from all this talk about guilt to touch on forgiveness, grace, and what it means to be a daughter of God. Being a Christian means that you are *in Christ*. Being in Christ is permanent—you don't jump in and out of grace depending on how righteous you are in any given moment. You are in grace when you are at your spiritual best, and you are *still* in grace when you are at your spiritual worst. Jesus doesn't abandon you and stop cleansing you the moment you sin—if anything, that's when he rolls up his sleeves and gets to work!

When you become a Christian, you become God's child and enter into grace. And God wants you to *enjoy* that grace. God doesn't want his daughters living in fear.

You have not received a spirit that makes you fearful slaves. Instead, you received God's Spirit when he adopted you as his own children. Now we call him, "Abba, Father."
ROMANS 8:15, NLT

I don't know what your earthly father is like, but I know this: loving fathers don't kick their kids out of the house (or off the tennis courts) the minute they make a mistake. Sure, they teach them some life lessons; yes, they help them grow and change, but never for one moment do they stop adoring their daughters. Not for one second do they consider pushing them away.

You are loved by your heavenly Father, period. Whether you hit the tennis ball or totally whiff it. Whether you have a God-honoring day or a terrible day. Whether you sin a dozen times this week or a dozen times every minute of every day this week. God loves you through your growing pains and mistakes—and he always will.

The next time you feel guilty, keep these truths in mind:

- God gives us guilty feelings (godly sorrow) to serve a purpose: to inspire change.
- You'll know you're dealing with godly sorrow if it nudges you toward good change (repentance) and inspires you to be more like Jesus.
- Healthy repentance leads to joy, peace, and confidence.
- You'll know you're dealing with worldly sorrow if it lasts too long and hurts you. It might even turn into phantom guilt.
- Once guilty feelings stop inspiring you to change and begin tormenting and paralyzing you, they have become worldly sorrow, and they are no longer useful or godly. It's time for them to leave.

THE BIGGEST WORD IN THE WORLD

Don't be fooled: *grace* may look like a little word—five teeny letters—but it's the biggest word in the world. It's big enough to cover all sins—past sins, today's sins, and every sin in your future. And it's big enough to do that for every single person who has lived before us, every person who lives today, and every person who ever will live.

And guess what? Your sins don't surprise God. Let's say you mess up one day for the umpteenth time that week; God doesn't smack a palm to his forehead and say, "Wow, I didn't know this girl was going to be such a handful." God's love is big enough and his grace is powerful enough to cover everything life throws at us—and everything we throw at him. From messy mistakes to dumb decisions to badly hit balls, he'll love us—and forgive us—through it all.

FEELING YOUR WAY FORWARD

Journal Prompts

1. When you experience worldly sorrow, what does it feel like? What kinds of thoughts does Satan whisper to you?
2. How does grace affect your relationship with God? Your relationship with other people?
3. Describe a time when you repented—made a change for good in your life. What helped you change, and how did you feel afterward?

Prayer Prompt

Oh, what joy for those
    whose disobedience is forgiven,
    whose sin is put out of sight!

Yes, what joy for those
whose record the LORD has cleared of guilt,
    whose lives are lived in complete honesty!
When I refused to confess my sin,
    my body wasted away,
    and I groaned all day long.
Day and night your hand of discipline was heavy on me.
My strength evaporated like water in the summer heat.
Finally, I confessed all my sins to you
    and stopped trying to hide my guilt.
I said to myself, "I will confess my rebellion to the LORD."
And you forgave me! All my guilt is gone.

PSALM 32:1-5, NLT

Lifelines

Five Scriptures about grace:

1. Ephesians 1:3-8
2. Ephesians 2:8-10
3. 2 Timothy 2:1
4. Romans 8:1-2
5. Romans 5:1-2

CHAPTER 12

ALL THE SWOONS

I'm sixteen, sitting in a New Jersey movie theater watching a romantic comedy play out on the screen. The heroine stalks-slash-follows her would-be true love to Italy. (*Of course* he's in Italy—I mean, who can find true love in New Jersey?) After multiple mis-adventures, she finally stumbles into love—but not till the final scene, when her *real* true love (not the guy she's been chasing) chases *her* down in the airport just as she's about to board the flight home. Yep, they're going to live happily—and sappily—ever after.

The credits roll, and as all the other moviegoers file out, I linger in my seat, hugging my empty popcorn tub. Sighing, swooning, *feeling*. Tingling with leftover laughter and the satisfaction of a happy ending, but there's more—so much more—swirling inside. The threads are so tangled it's hard to even identify them all: a deep-down ache of longing, a hint of loneliness, a touch of inse-curity, a bit of sadness, a shadow of fear.

My heart flings desperate questions out into the universe, and I turn them into a prayer I feel kind of embarrassed about: *God, will anyone ever love me enough to chase me down in an airport? Am I worth chasing? Will anyone ever look at me the way he looks at her—all puppy dog eyes and "You're the most beautiful thing I've ever seen and I'd be lost without you"? Am I beautiful? Is there such thing as a soul mate—and if there is, did you make one for me, God? Someone who loves Shakespeare and sunsets and cheeseburgers and chocolate?*

But you know what? Looking back, that prayer wasn't embarrassing at all. I'm glad I prayed it. It was honest and raw—and the desires and questions it expressed were part of the way God wired me.

Yes, you read that right: the desire to love and be loved is put inside us by God—it's an intrinsic part of who we are. Way back in the Garden of Eden, when God made the very first person, God declared, "It is not good for the man to be alone" (Genesis 2:18). We aren't meant to live solitary lives! God knows that we need people to walk through life with. Some people are called to be single—to live a fulfilling, happy, godly life in the context of friends and community. Other people are called to serve God within the context of marriage and a family. But all of us, whether single or married, are wired with a need to love and be loved, to be connected to other human beings.

So what does this mean for *you*—a Christian girl trying to honor God with her choices and relationships? When the time comes, what should you be looking for in a guy? How can you manage your feelings about boys? What do you do when you think you're in love?

Before we talk about finding true love on earth, let's remember an important truth. You already have the most important love of all, the truest love of all: the love of God.

THE TRUEST LOVE

You, beautiful girl, are already deeply loved. You already have someone who adores you, delights in you, wants to share life with you. No boy—not even the godliest, most thoughtful, and (seemingly) perfect of human boys—can ever fill the God-shaped space in your heart.

Before you try to develop a romantic relationship, it's important to fill yourself up with the love of God. Read Scriptures about God's love over and over until you start to believe them. Work on developing a relationship with God—not just going through the motions, but talking to him throughout the day, celebrating happy moments with him, sharing your tears, seeking his help in all your daily struggles. And remember these truths:

- Boys will sometimes make mistakes; God never will.
- Boys will sometimes misunderstand you; God never will.
- Boys will sometimes be unaware of your needs; God never will.
- Boys will sometimes forget things they should remember; God never will.
- Boys will sometimes lie; God never will.
- Boys will sometimes let you down; God never will.

Remembering these truths takes a lot of pressure off a relationship. It frees you to give and receive love without expecting a guy to fill the places in your soul only God can fill.

ONCE UPON A TIME, IN THE LIFE OF A BIG FEELER

The student worship night has ended. While all my friends hang out and have fun in the sanctuary, I've retreated to one of the Sunday school classrooms, the one with the pastel Noah's ark border, trying to catch up on schoolwork. Sitting cross-legged on the carpeted floor, I am a stressed-out island surrounded by a sea of school supplies: battered green backpack, barely-read copy of *The Odyssey*, notebooks, flash cards, pens, highlighters. *Behind, behind, I'm so behind.*

Guilt and shame swirl inside, an eddy with tornado potential. How did I let this happen? Fear enters the mix as my old nemesis, Worst-Case-Scenario Disorder, rears its ridiculous head: *What if I fail this class? If I fail, I'll fall apart and lose all hope and ambition and end up scooping ice cream for the rest of my life and—*

"Knock, knock." My thoughts blink off, momentarily stunned, like a squirrel in the street.

Football Boy is standing just inside the door. Leaning against the doorframe all casual and *I-know-I'm-cute-so-sue-me.*

My heart does a cartwheel.

Fighting the dopey grin that wants to hijack my mouth whenever he's around, I spare him a tight-lipped, no-I-don't-think-you're-the-most-beautiful-human-alive smile, and brace myself: *Here's the part where he flashes me a stiff grin and then rushes off to find the person he was actually looking for.*

"Hi," he says, flashing me a totally not-stiff grin.

"Hi?" I say, then force my eyeballs not to roll. *Why'd you have to tack a question mark onto that "hi," Elizabeth? Just say hi! Exclamation point!*

Then: *Did he come in here on purpose? Was he looking for me?*

The eddy of feelings reverses direction, a different kind of stress: a swirl of lovesick longing.

Don't get your hopes up, Elizabeth—he's probably looking for someone else. He's always looking for someone else.

I dig into my bag and shove a piece of gum into my mouth, my only resistance against the flood of dumb comments trying to bubble up my throat. *Don't babble, just chew. Ignore him and go back to your books.*

But then Football Boy plops down beside me, folding his mile-long legs up and hugging them to his chest. Settling in for a chat.

We're sitting alone in a room.

Just the two of us.

I half-choke on my gum, making a horrifying gargly noise, which I try to cover with a cough.

"So . . . whatcha doin'?" he says, and his Georgia drawl does something squirmy to my stomach.

"Oh, you know, beating myself up for procrastinating—which is really just another way of procrastinating. So . . . the usual." I give what I know is a borderline flirtatious grin, then barely suppress an I-hate-myself groan. *Could you have* possibly *given a more dorky response, Elizabeth? Now he thinks you're a vocabulary show-off and a school nerd. So basically, you're a double nerd. Not to mention a very bad flirt—and isn't flirting a sin?* Guilt-tinged worry prods at my conscience.

I duck my head and start shoving my stuff rather violently into my bag. *Must shut this conversation down before I say more stupid things.* I wait for The Boy to get bored and leave, but he stretches out his legs and leans back on his elbows, like he plans to stay awhile. Confused, I slow down my packing.

He flicks a finger at my imitation Doc Martens. "New boots?"

My cheeks, foul traitors, blaze with pleasure. *He noticed!* "Yep," I say, trying to affect a casual shrug. "They're really comfortable. And they were on sale, so . . . yeah." *Babbling. UGH.*

My eyes dart up to meet his. Usually this is when we both look away—he because he's waving hello to another football player or sporty girl, I because I'm trying not to let him see me swoon—but tonight he holds my gaze, and I dare to hold his back. His eyes are brown, coffee brown—no, chocolate brown. No, coffee *with* chocolate brown. No matter, I adore both. It must be a sign.

"I like them," he says, sliding me one of his side-smiles.

"Thanks." I drop my eyes back to my boots, hoping he doesn't realize my heart has sprouted wings.

He stretches, yawns. "Well, I guess it's time to head out."

"Yeah," I say. "About that time. Can I still get a ride?"

He smacks my shoulder. "Always." He winks.

My heart bursts out of my chest and zings around the room in a hallelujah dance. *He said "always"! Like a little promise. We're totally getting married.*

I shake my head, trying to calm my chaotic thoughts, crush my idiotic hopes. *Don't be ridiculous, Elizabeth.* I stumble to my feet, fumble my backpack onto my shoulder, and traipse behind him, new boots squeaking, already planning how I'm going to call my best friend, Sara, and spend four hours breaking down every nuance of this four-minute conversation. After that I can get back to my regularly scheduled guilt trip.

* * *

Maybe you're a big feeler like I am, and you know exactly what this kind of be-still-my-heart scenario feels like. Or maybe you're more level-headed about love and you like to take your time: you scrutinize, analyze, and theorize before letting your heart feel too much. However you respond to the fluttery feelings, we can all agree: they make life complicated-delightful-amazing-agonizing-confusing-terrifying-embarrassing-thrilling. Which is, in fact, an actual feeling.

It can be tough to think straight when emotions like that hit! And it's not like we always know they're coming, either. One day we're walking down the hall, feeling just fine, thank you very much, and then in walks Mr. Handsome with his Perfect Everything—sensitive eyes, sideways smile, swoopy hair blowing in the school air-conditioning—and our hearts flip cartwheels as our brains turn to mashed potatoes. That's why it helps to think and pray about romance and crushes and dating ahead of time, so we're a little more prepared when swoony feelings come.

So how can a Christian girl use biblical principles to direct her romantic feelings and dating life in a way that honors God?

WHAT THE BIBLE SAYS ABOUT DATING

Are you ready for some surprising news? The Bible doesn't say anything about boyfriends or dating! Not exactly—not directly. The Bible does have things to say about romance in general, and it offers plenty of guidelines for marriage and family life, but you're not going to find a section in Scripture titled "10 Qualities to Look for in a Boyfriend" or "How to Know He's a Godly Guy." You won't find a dating rulebook or a list of dos and don'ts.

The courtship rituals of people in biblical times were dramatically different from ours. That doesn't mean the Bible can't guide our relationship choices, but we can't just look up the word *dating* in Scripture. We have to study more deeply to understand God's will for romance. If we're going to conduct our dating lives—and one day our marriages—in a godly way, we have to search the Bible for principles to direct us toward God's big-picture will for our hearts and relationships.

So does God care who you date? Of course he does! As your doting Father, God cares about *everything* in your life. He cares about your family life, your grades, your sports, your friendships, your dating life—your entire life. God is not the Cosmic Killjoy in the Sky, brandishing his fatherly baseball bat at all the boys you think are cute. He is a loving Father who wants to see his daughter happy and confident and loved the way she deserves.

If God's plan for you involves marriage, he wants you, his beloved daughter, to marry a godly man who will respect and adore you. And since dating is part of the way our society prepares us for marriage, God cares a great deal about who we date, how we date, and how we choose our boyfriends . . . and eventually our spouses.

When you and your parents agree that you can start dating, godly principles can help guide your decisions. So what does God want for marriages and families, and how can those guidelines point us toward smart dating decisions?

- God wants godly people to marry other godly people. We should marry inside the faith (see 1 Corinthians 7:39; 2 Corinthians 6:14-18; see also the ancient-but-still-romantic story of Isaac and Rebekah in Genesis 24).
- God wants husbands and wives to love each other deeply and forever (see Ephesians 5:21-33; Matthew 19:1-9). Of course, we know that even in Christian homes, heartache and divorce can happen. But these verses show us the kind of commitment and security God longs for his children to experience and enjoy in their marriages.
- God wants parents to partner together to raise their children in his ways (see Deuteronomy 6:4-9; Ephesians 5:21–6:4; Colossians 3:18-21).

TIPS FOR FINDING THE RIGHT GUY

What do these principles tell us? How can they help us make good choices when it comes to dating? Our number-one priority when we think about who to date should be finding a godly guy. And finding a godly guy is going to affect your dating life in a few key ways:

You're going to have to be pickier than some of your friends.

You're not just looking for a charming boy or a cute boy—you're looking for someone with substance. Faith. Conviction. Someone who loves God as much as you do.

And keep this in mind: you are a daughter of God, a daughter of the King, which makes you a princess. And princesses don't date bozos. Princesses are picky. They have extremely high standards.

You might have to be more patient than other girls.

Since godly guys are harder to find than guys who are merely good looking or nice, you may need to be patient and wait longer than you'd like to. You may need to be more patient than your friends who aren't as concerned with dating godly boys.

You'll have to be intentional about dating.

If you find a boy you're interested in, you'll need to take some time and get to know him before you get in too deep. Ask questions, have real conversations, get to know his life and his faith.

You don't have to figure out forever.

I know we're talking a lot about being thoughtful and intentional, but dating is just dating. It's not marriage. Dating is a way to dip your toes into the romantic waters, trying to figure out how to swim in this new place. As much as I was a hopeless romantic who wanted to know who I was going to marry when I was sixteen, I wasn't ready to choose a husband yet. I hardly knew my own heart—how could I know someone else's? How could I give my heart away when I didn't know what was in it?

I'm not saying you can't find your future spouse early in life, only that it's fine—even good—to take a "let's just have fun and get to know each other" approach and leave the Big Serious Lifetime Commitments for a little later in life!

Pray about your dating life.

Remember, the desire to be in love is not a bad thing—God designed us to long for love and companionship. So when you feel that lonely feeling, know that this is just part of the way God created you!

Don't be afraid to talk to God about what you feel, what you want, and what you're looking for. I used to pray specific prayers: "God, please help me find someone who really loves you and who likes movies and books like I do. I kind of like dark hair and big muscles, but I'm flexible." I think those honest conversations made God smile—and maybe even laugh!

When you begin to have feelings for someone, don't be embarrassed to pray about those feelings. Tell God what you feel, and ask him for guidance and clarity. Your prayers aren't boring or embarrassing to God. They're a big deal to you, so they're a big

Characteristics to Look For in a Guy

- He loves God first. He doesn't just go to church or youth group; he has a relationship with God.
- He has fun . . . in ways that honor God.
- He talks to you about his faith and asks you about yours. (Not all the time—you don't have to feel like you're hanging out with a pastor or something—but spiritual topics should sometimes come up in your conversations!)
- He respects you and doesn't push sexual boundaries. He listens to you and shows a willingness to change if you tell him that something he's doing (or something you're doing together) makes you feel uncomfortable or guilty.

Questions to Ask Yourself When Deciding to Date Someone

- What character traits do I like in this person?
- What character traits do I admire in this person?
- Does he love God? What evidence do I see of his relationship with God? (Hint: going to church or being part of a youth group doesn't automatically mean he's spiritual. I've met a lot of knuckleheads who go to church!)
- Do I like the person I am when I am around him, or do I change who I am to try to impress him?

deal to your Father. He wants to hear from you, and he wants to help you make wise choices.

CAN I CHOOSE WHO I LOVE?

How many times have you heard someone say something like, "I can't help who I fall in love with"? This idea is hammered into our hearts by movies and books. They make it seem like romance happens when we are inevitably, irresistibly drawn to a certain person. We don't choose our love—love chooses us. Nothing we do can stop the big-feelings train.

Of course, romance begins with attraction and involves a lot of emotion. But there's a key difference: the distinction between attraction and love. *Attraction* is an instinctive reaction. Maybe you're attracted to someone because you think he's good looking. Or maybe you're drawn to his personality—you just like being around him. Attraction gives you fluttery, flustered feelings, aka The Swoon. Your stomach gets twisty, your breath comes fast, your cheeks grow hot, your tongue gets tied—or worse, your mouth babbles idiotic things.

But attraction is not love. It can be the beginning of love, the spark that leads to love . . . but love involves building respect and trust. Eventually, that love may grow into commitment. This doesn't happen in an instant, the moment you spot a chiseled jaw and stormy eyes across the room. Attraction is instantaneous; love takes time.

Attraction is a thrilling, intoxicating feeling, and it's not wrong to be attracted to other people. However, we also have to engage our *brains* when attraction hits. We can't just let attraction sweep us away. We have to think, pray, and make choices.

One of my favorite verses about romance is Song of Songs 8:4: "Daughters of Jerusalem, I charge you: Do not arouse or awaken love until it so desires." I have always taken this verse to mean that we shouldn't allow love to take over in our hearts before its time—before we're ready. This Scripture also reminds me that we have a *choice* in when we awaken love in our hearts. Attraction grows when we feed it. If we realize we're attracted to a person who doesn't bring out our spiritual best, we can intentionally redirect our thoughts, our feelings, and the places where we spend our time. When we do this, we can take charge of our feelings.

When I was eighteen, I acted in a scene with a boy from my acting class. Our teacher assigned us an intensely emotional scene, and after a few rehearsals, I started feeling . . . interested. Fluttery. Attracted. There was a problem: this boy was not a Christian. I don't think he even believed in God. I knew a relationship with him wouldn't be part of God's plan for me, but my feelings disagreed with God's plan. I had a choice to make: Would I feed these feelings or shift my focus somewhere else? It took talks with friends and with God, but eventually I redirected my feelings, and when the play ended, we parted ways as friends, nothing more.

Through that experience, I learned that I shouldn't read too much into my feelings of attraction or desire. We may not be able to choose who gives us the flutters—remember, physical attraction is an automatic response, more about your hormones than your heart—but giving our hearts to someone in a romantic relationship is something different altogether.

With God's help, we can choose who we love. We can't always choose who we are instinctively attracted to, but we can choose who we give our hearts to. If you ever have confusing feelings about someone—maybe someone who isn't godly or isn't a good influence—I encourage you to open up to a parent or trusted mentor. They can help you think through, work through, and pray through whatever you're feeling so you can make godly choices.

We started out this chapter in a movie theater with sixteen-year-old me. Fast-forward a number of years, and I'm a mom with teenage daughters of my own. I've found my Romeo, and believe it or not, I won his heart in . . . wait for it . . . Paris, France! (Who says God didn't hear my prayer that day in the movie theater?)

I don't know when my daughters will find the men who will be worthy of their hearts, but I trust that the Lord will work out his good plans for them. Our heavenly Father sees each of my girls, knows them, loves them—even better than I do—and he has wonderful plans for their future . . . and yours.

I pray that you save your princess dreams and your precious heart for the right guy—a godly guy, a prince. And when he does come—whether you find him in Italy, France, New Jersey, or the church down the street—I pray you turn to your Father in heaven to guide your choices. And when God finally brings your prince into your life, I pray he treats you like a queen.

FEELING YOUR WAY FORWARD

Journal Prompts

1. Describe the kind of person you hope to marry one day.
2. Do you feel comfortable talking to God about your hopes for romance and your dating life? Why or why not?
3. How would you define a godly relationship?

Prayer Prompt

I have seen you in the sanctuary
    and beheld your power and your glory.
Because your love is better than life,
    my lips will glorify you.
I will praise you as long as I live,
    and in your name I will lift up my hands.

PSALM 63:2-4

Lifelines

Five Scriptures on trusting God's plans and timing in your life:

1. Ephesians 1:11-12
2. Romans 8:28-30
3. Proverbs 3:5-6
4. Galatians 6:8-9
5. Jeremiah 17:7-8

CHAPTER 13

SOCIAL MEDIA: THE GOOD, THE BAD, AND THE AIRBRUSHED

I'm scrolling through my Instagram feed. Every picture is perfectly lit, possibly airbrushed, and definitely frameworthy. There's a woman with skin so flawless it actually glows, strolling down the street in an adorable (*adorable* meaning "I could never afford it") outfit. A laughing group of girls with matching suntans shares a group hug on a pristine beach. A gorgeous couple gazes dreamily into one another's eyes. After about ten minutes of scrolling, my stomach has folded in on itself, and my shoulders feel like they're carrying a backpack of bricks. *What's going on?* I ask myself. *Why am I upset? I was happy ten minutes ago!*

The truth is, my scrolling has left me feeling *less than*: less happy, less beautiful, less interesting, less intelligent, less spiritual, less put together, less talented, less successful, less loved. All these other people seem to be living thrilling, joy-packed lives. They're in love, they have a posse of adoring friends (who all look like supermodels), their families are happy and perfect, they have money to travel to exotic beaches, and they have profound things to say about life, all while wearing trendy clothes. Me? I'm just living my boring, penny-pinching, off-brand life at home in my sweatpants. A life I liked and was relatively happy with until ten minutes ago.

Have you ever been there? You log on to social media, looking for a break or maybe something to chase away boredom . . . and *wham*. Suddenly you're feeling all the bad feels—all the insecure, jealous, ungrateful, unhappy, FOMO feels.

Of course social media isn't all bad. Other times your experience is just the opposite: maybe you're feeling down, and you read a post that's uplifting or inspiring. And sometimes social media gives us more than inspiration: I have social media to thank for several of my dearest friendships—and, in my brother's case, it introduced him to his wife!

Social media isn't inherently good or bad—it's neutral. It can be a fountain of good or an ocean of evil; it can be used by God— or used by Satan. It can be a catalyst for change, a spring of hope, a tool for good; but it can also be a source of hatred, division, and deceit. It can help us feel connected or chain us to our phones. For better or worse, social media is a cultural force, a constant presence. And it's not going anywhere.

In your lifetime, you're bound to navigate a dizzying number of social platforms, technologies, and ways to connect, and you'll have to make countless decisions along the way about who you want to be and how you want to live. Those choices will have a profound effect on our emotional health and spiritual well-being, so the sooner you begin making those choices on purpose, the better!

In this chapter we'll discuss three guiding principles to help you use social media in ways that reflect your faith, honor God, and help you lead an emotionally healthy life:

1. Shine for Christ.
2. Post on purpose.
3. Take charge.

Let's take a closer look at each of these three principles.

SHINE FOR CHRIST

How should Christians view social media and conduct themselves online? Let's begin by thinking about who Christians are called to be in general.

We're called to be like Jesus wherever we go.

> You are the light of the world—like a city on a hilltop
> that cannot be hidden. No one lights a lamp and then
> puts it under a basket. Instead, a lamp is placed on a
> stand, where it gives light to everyone in the house. In the
> same way, let your good deeds shine out for all to see, so
> that everyone will praise your heavenly Father.
> MATTHEW 5:14-16, NLT

A light to the world. A city on a hill. When people look at us—including our social media profiles—do we reflect Christ?

We're called to grow in the fruit of the Spirit as we grow in our walk with God.

> The Holy Spirit produces this kind of fruit in our
> lives: love, joy, peace, patience, kindness, goodness,
> faithfulness, gentleness, and self-control. There is no
> law against these things!
> Those who belong to Christ Jesus have nailed the
> passions and desires of their sinful nature to his cross
> and crucified them there. Since we are living by the

Spirit, let us follow the Spirit's leading in every part of
our lives.
GALATIANS 5:22-25, NLT

In everything we do, say, and post, let's seek to cultivate more
fruit that makes God happy: more love, joy, peace, patience, kindness, goodness, faithfulness, gentleness, and self-control.

We're called to set our minds on things above.

Fix your thoughts on what is true, and honorable, and
right, and pure, and lovely, and admirable. Think about
things that are excellent and worthy of praise.
PHILIPPIANS 4:8, NLT

Christians are called to direct our thoughts and desires on spiritual things. Our minds and hearts are meant for something higher
than just the latest trending hashtag. It's not that we can't have fun
talking about movies or books or fashion or food or other interests. Those things can be a fun part of our lives—but they can't
be our lives. God calls Christians to set our hearts and hopes on
heaven—and on him.

POST ON PURPOSE

Here's one of my favorite lifeline verses to help guide our words
and choices on social media:

Let the message about Christ, in all its richness, fill
your lives. Teach and counsel each other with all the
wisdom he gives . . . *And whatever you do or say, do it as
a representative of the Lord Jesus, giving thanks through him
to God the Father.*
COLOSSIANS 3:16-17, NLT (EMPHASIS ADDED)

Let's take a closer look at how this Scripture can guide our lives on social media:

Let the message of Christ . . . fill your lives: Do you have room for the message of Christ in your mind, heart, and life, or is social media taking up so much mental and emotional space that Jesus is getting crowded out?

Is the message of Christ filling you so richly that it can't help but pour out of you in the words and pictures you post? That doesn't mean that everything you post has to be overtly spiritual, but it does need to be God-honoring. Whether you're interacting with someone online or in person, you want to reflect God's character in the way you conduct yourself.

Here's a good self-test: let's say you make a new friend on social media, and they only know you through your social media accounts. Would they be surprised to find out you are a Christian?

Whatever you do or say, do it as a representative of the Lord Jesus: Everything we do or say needs to reflect positively on Christ. I know—that's an intense expectation, isn't it? Jesus' call doesn't change just because we're online. Christian principles should guide our choices, relationships, interactions, and words— both in person and on screens. (Here's a good rule of thumb: if you wouldn't say something to a person's face, don't say it to them online.) I'm not writing this to make you feel paranoid or guilty but to help you to be thoughtful. To think (and even pray and seek advice) before you post.

Some people on social media are invited to be "brand ambassadors" for certain products and services. They post images and advertisements to point people to certain products and make those products seem attractive. Well, guess what? As Christians, you and I are "brand ambassadors" for Jesus. When people look at the words and images we share, we represent him.

TAKE CHARGE

When I decided I wanted to write books, I was told that I needed to be active on social media. I dove in with all of my big-feeling heart, thinking, *This will be fun! I can encourage other Christians and even share my faith!* I started with the best of intentions—godly ones, even!—but I was soon caught up in a current I couldn't escape, being dragged out to sea, farther and farther from my family and the life I wanted to lead. I found myself checking my social media accounts multiple times an hour, posting and commenting and liking and friending and sharing and thumbs-upping and emoji-ing. The notifications pummeled me All. Day. Long.

Conversations like this started happening with my husband:

Kevin: "Hey, Elizabeth, can you come help me with my grad school paper?"

Me, not looking up from the screen: "Mm-hmm. Just a sec." My fingers continue to fly, typing responses to eight different comment threads.

Five minutes later . . .

Kevin, sounding slightly annoyed: "Elizabeth? Were you going to come look at this?"

Me, looking up with glazed eyes: "What?"

Kevin, waving his papers: "My paper? Were you going to help me?"

Me, my cheeks flooding with heat: "Of course! Sorry. I just . . . this message . . . this girl needed advice. Sorry."

I walk over to the couch and sit beside Kevin. He says, "I'd love your thoughts on the thesis. I wanted to talk about—"

Ding. The sound of a new comment.

I try to ignore it.

Ding. Another comment.

My eyes flick away from Kevin's face and steal a glance at my screen. I wonder if the girl is responding to my advice. If she did, I need to respond right away. Or maybe that big blogger responded to my share, and I need to . . .

Kevin clears his throat and I blink, looking at him—actually *seeing* him—again. His face is covered in hurt.

Guilt squeezes a hard fist around my heart, and I realize, *Something has to change. I have to change.*

* * *

Does that scenario feel familiar? Have you ever been where I was? Are you there now? Maybe you've never spent much time thinking about your relationship with social media before. Maybe, like me, you created an account, and the liking and friending and following pulled you into their powerful current and you've been caught in the flow ever since. Maybe you've gotten a handle on it, and now you're happily treading water in a happy, healthy place. Or maybe the rip current is pulling you out into the deep end and you're barely keeping your head above water.

My early experiences with social media taught me some painful lessons. I realized I had to become intentional about my social media life. In other words, I couldn't just mindlessly go with the flow—I needed to think about my relationship with social media. I needed to take charge of the relationship. And I use the word *relationship* here because, like human relationships, our interactions with social media involve give-and-take.

Social media gives you some things: connection, information, inspiration, entertainment, opportunities. And whether you realize it or not, social media also takes some things from you: your time, your energy, your privacy, your creativity, your photos, your personal stories.

Social media is like a bucket with a hole in the bottom: the more water you pour in, the more water pours out. You can stand there trying to fill that bucket All. Day. Long. You can turn on the hose as high as it goes. But that bucket is never going to get full, no matter what you do—it's never going to be "satisfied."

Social media never takes breaks—and it never gives you one either. It never turns itself off so you can go to sleep early or take a

Quiz: Is Social Media Taking Over Your Life?

Grab a piece of paper and take a few minutes to think about your social media life and how you feel about it. Write down your answers to these questions:

- How many social media platforms are you on?
- How much time do you spend on social media each day?
- How many notifications do you get from social media per day? (Give your best guess. You could write down a number for the whole day or a number per hour.)
- List each social media platform you use, and write down why you're on it and why you like it (or dislike it!).
- How do you feel about your current social media usage? Happy? Connected? Annoyed? Burdened? Guilty? Overwhelmed? Neutral?
- How do you think God feels about your social media habits? Why do you think he feels that way?
- What do you think a healthy relationship with social media should look like?
- In what ways does your feeling type affect your interactions with social media?
- If you could change one thing about your social media habits, what would it be?

Did you learn some things about yourself? I would encourage you to pray about the things you wrote down, share your thoughts with a parent or mentor, and make some decisions about any changes you need to make.

Quiz: Should You Join That New Platform?

Let's say all your friends are telling you, "We all just joined this Amazing New Platform! Everybody's on there! Big Exciting Things are happening! You should join us so you don't get left out of all the fun!"

Before you join any new platform, it's helpful to ask yourself these questions:

- Why do I want to join this platform?
- How do I think this platform will benefit me? What will it give me?
- What will this platform take from me?
- What are the potential drawbacks or dangers I might encounter on this platform?
- If I join this platform, what boundaries, time limits, or healthy habits do I need to put in place?
- How do my parents feel about me joining?

Discuss your answers with your parents, and make a decision together about whether this new platform will add positive things to your life and bring out the best in you.

Quiz: Has a Social Media Platform Crossed into Creepy Territory?

Sometimes we enjoy being on a platform for a while, but then things start to change. We start feeling less happy and connected, further away from God, more burdened and stressed, or just vaguely *icky*. Those feelings are signs that it may be time to make some changes, take a break, or sign off altogether.

Take a look at these statements and ask yourself if they are true or false:

	TRUE	FALSE
I don't like the way I feel when I'm engaging on this platform.		
Being on this platform makes me feel bad about myself— my appearance, my friendships, my house, my possessions, my life.		
I feel guilty about my interactions on this platform.		
The relationships I've cultivated on this platform are unhealthy or ungodly.		
I experience bullying, unkindness, peer pressure, or shaming on this platform.		
I'm getting friended or followed by creepy people who make me feel uncomfortable or unsafe.		

If you answered "true" to even one of these statements, it's time for a conversation with God, your parents, and your mentors. They can help you to decide if you need to make some changes, take a break, or sign off from this platform altogether.

mental break or go on vacation or spend time with God and your family. It's always there, relentlessly calling, "Come read this post! Like this image! Comment on this thread! See what you've been missing!"

Social media will always want more from you. More of your time. More of your pictures. More of your energy. More of your secrets. You will never get a social media notification that says, "Hey, you've spent enough time on me today. Why don't you go for a walk or practice the piano or hang out with someone in person?" Nope. It will always demand more. So *you* have to decide when you've had enough.

Because of this, we have to take charge. Taking charge means we stop, step back, and think. We ask ourselves questions and make choices.

CONNECTED, NOT CHAINED

It's time to get practical. What are some "best practices" you can put into place to help you develop a healthy, happy relationship with social media? Let's talk about strategies, schedules, and breaks.

Strategies

Every family has different perspectives on social media. Maybe you feel like your parents are super strict. Or maybe your parents don't understand or care about social media, so they stay hands off and let you do what you want. Either way, I encourage you to invite your parents into your decisions about social media as an ongoing conversation.

New platforms are always popping up, and as you mature and change, your needs and desires and friend groups (and temptations!) will change too. What works for you for a while may not work later. A platform that you love for a while can become an unhealthy place later. And that's why the conversation needs to be ongoing.

Schedules

Regardless of your age, I recommend setting some time limits for your social media usage. This isn't just something teens need to do—we *all* need to take charge of our social media habits so they don't take over our lives.

This will look different for each person, but just to give you an idea, here are three limits I've set up for myself:

- No push notifications for social media on my phone. I don't want to get dinged every time something happens. If I want to know what's happening on a platform, I just log in and check.
- I generally stay off social media when I'm with my family or friends. That allows me to be fully *with* the people I'm with.
- I rarely log on to social media on the weekends.

You will probably settle on different guidelines for yourself— maybe for you, the weekends are the only time you *can* get on social media because schooldays are so busy!—but I hope you'll come up with some boundaries that make sense for you and your family. You might try experimenting with different schedules to see what works best—what allows you to feel *connected* to the digital world but not *chained* to it.

Breaks

The apostle Paul wrote:

> You say, "I am allowed to do anything"—but not everything is good for you. And even though "I am allowed to do anything," I must not become a slave to anything.
>
> 1 CORINTHIANS 6:12, NLT

In context, Paul was writing about sexual sin, yet the spirit of his words can apply to other areas of our lives. We don't want to be slaves to anything—and how easy it is to become enslaved by social media.

Every so often it's helpful to do a social media "detox"—to just take a few days or even weeks off altogether. Sometimes our brains and hearts need a little time to refresh and reset.

If the idea of signing off social media for a time makes you feel panicky, that's a good sign you might need a break! I promise, you'll still have a social life and friends if you take some time away from social media.

Taking time away to "detox" allows us several benefits:

- It gives us time to unplug and reset our hearts and habits.
- It frees up time for family and friends.
- It frees us from constant distractions and multitasking.
- It opens up space in our minds for God and his Word.
- It offers us perspective, giving us the distance we need to recognize any changes we need to make in our social media habits.

* * *

Whew. Social media gives us a lot to think about, doesn't it? Let's be clear about something: we won't get social media "right" all the time. We all post some things we later realize were mistakes. At times we may find our thoughts too consumed with our image or followers or reputation. But hey, we're human, and we're all still learning and growing.

And you know? I think that's the secret to thriving in life—including the digital life: we don't have to get it perfect all the time; we just have to keep learning. Keep growing. Keep thinking. Keep choosing to live (and post) on purpose.

FEELING YOUR WAY FORWARD

Journal Prompts

1. How do you feel about your relationship with social media? If you could change one thing, what would it be?
2. If someone only knows you from social media, how do you think they would describe you? How would you *want* people to describe your online personality?
3. Which of the following areas do you want to work on when it comes to social media: strategies, schedules, or breaks? What changes would you like to make?

Prayer Prompt

Give praise to the LORD, proclaim his name;
    make known among the nations what he has done,
    and proclaim that his name is exalted.
Sing to the LORD, for he has done glorious things;
    let this be known to all the world.

ISAIAH 12:4-5

Lifelines

Five Scriptures about setting a godly example:

1. Colossians 3:16-17
2. Colossians 4:5-6
3. 2 Corinthians 5:20
4. 1 Peter 2:11-12
5. Philippians 1:27

CHAPTER 14

WHERE DO WE GO FROM HERE?

My parents tell me that on the day after I turned three, I turned to them, eyes brimming, lower lip trembling, and asked, "When will I be two again?"

Mom and Dad exchanged sentimental glances and said, "Never, honey. You'll never be two again."

As my sniffles built into sobs and my sobs amped up to wails, Mom and Dad frantically talked over each other, telling me all the wonderful things I had to look forward to now that I was three: "Now you can learn to ride a tricycle! Now you can sit in a booster seat! Now you can . . . uh . . . unwrap slices of cheese by yourself!" (This was a decidedly low point in their argument.)

But you know what? I'm really glad I didn't stay two forever. And I'm glad I didn't stay twelve or twenty-two either. Because growing is fun. Exciting. Adventurous. As Christians, that growth is even more fulfilling, because thanks to God's Spirit at work in us, we don't just grow older; we can also grow better. More Christlike. More faithful. More resilient. More confident in who God made us to be. More generous with our emotional and spiritual gifts.

As we near the end of this book, I pray you've already begun to see yourself growing. I pray that you're feeling more confident in the person God made you to be and loving the skin you live in—even if that skin is thinner (or thicker!) than you'd like it to be.

Maybe you've always viewed yourself as emotionally fragile—it doesn't take much for you to fall apart. I pray you've found some Scriptures, truths, and tools to help you handle big feelings with less freaking out and fear, more resilience and grace.

Maybe you've always struggled to love the person God designed you to be—you wish your feelings were bigger or smaller or just . . . different. I pray this book has helped you gain a better understanding of the beautiful soul God put inside you and the emotional gifts he is eager for you to share with others.

Maybe you've always felt frustrated by your resistance to feelings—the way you instinctively barricade the door of your heart whenever big feelings show up. I pray you are learning to identify and welcome your feelings, cracking open the door of your heart, and making yourself more vulnerable so you can connect more deeply with God and people.

I pray you have already seen some progress—*felt* some progress. But here's the thing to remember about spiritual growth: it's an imperfect process, and it takes time. Often way more time than we want it to. If you're a perfectionist-slash-guilt-prone soul like I am, then you may be thinking and feeling things like this: *I just read a whole book on feelings, so by the time I hit "The End," I should be handling my feelings better—and by "better" I mean "perfectly." I should be strong. Guilt-free. Doubt-free. Confident in God. Loving and kind and never jealous or insecure or petty in my friendships. Joyful and giving all the time, no matter what. Completely done with Panic Mode and freak-outs.*

And maybe, for about five everything-is-awesome minutes, you are all those things. But then life happens, old habits resurface, and you're crushed. *Did I learn anything at all?* you wonder. *Am I just a big fake? Or* (and here comes a tidal wave of I-can't-believe-I'm-thinking-this guilt) *does the Bible not actually work?*

I totally feel your pain, but please give yourself a break. Growth is a process. You will never be done growing! And don't just take it from me—take it from science. Even though you'll probably stop growing height-wise in your midteens, your brain won't finish developing until you're in your midtwenties. (Pardon the pun, but isn't that mind blowing?) Your brain hasn't finished maturing yet, so why would you expect yourself to have all of life and your feelings (and your faith!) totally figured out? God certainly doesn't expect that of you.

KEEP MATURING

The police officer tapped on the car window, and my dad rolled it down. The moment the window cracked open, a piercing wail blasted into the night, so loud the officer took a step back. Peering into the backseat, the cop saw a red-faced young girl—that would be me, back when I was three—sobbing and gasping for breath. My mom sat beside me, stroking my arm.

"Uh, license and registration, please," the officer stammered. "You were going a little fast there."

"Yeah," Dad mumbled. "Sorry. Just wanted to get my daughter home." He fumbled through his wallet and the glove compartment and finally produced the documents. The wailing climbed an octave, and both men flinched.

"What's wrong with your daughter?" the officer asked, examining the license through squinty eyes. "Is she—is she afraid of police officers?" He stumbled over his words, as if he felt guilty.

"No . . . we took her to the movies," Dad said, his mystified expression seeming to say, *We were trying to do something fun.*

The cop raised an eyebrow. "Did she fall down on the way out or something?"

"No." Dad pressed the heels of his hands against his forehead. "She thought the ending was sad."

At this, my wails reached a pitch usually only attainable by dog whistles and teakettles.

The officer grimaced. "You know what?" He thrust the license and papers back through the window. "Just get that poor kid home. And drive more slowly this time."

Mumbling a sheepish "Thanks," Dad pulled away, not bothering to roll up the window. My weeping trailed the car like a siren.

The story of "The Time I Cried So Hard I Got My Dad Out of a Speeding Ticket" has become legend in my family. Moments like this were early indicators that big feelings were going to play a big part in my life and that I was going to need to learn how to manage those feelings as I matured.

But you know what? I did grow . . . and I'm still growing today. I haven't mastered my feelings (I still cry at movies and cheesy commercials, although I haven't scared any police officers lately), but I've come a long way from that tearful car ride.

God has shown me great patience along the way—and he'll do the same for you. All he asks is that you love him, give him your heart, and keep taking steps forward in your faith. They don't have to be leaps and bounds—they can be wobbly baby steps, with occasional face-plants thrown in for good measure. Even if you're new to faith and growth, God's Word can help you to mature over time.

> Like newborn babies, you must crave pure spiritual milk
> so that you will *grow into* a full experience of salvation.
> Cry out for this nourishment, now that you have had a
> taste of the Lord's kindness.

You are coming to Christ, who is the living cornerstone of God's temple. He was rejected by people, but he was chosen by God for great honor.

And you are living stones that God *is building* into his spiritual temple.

1 PETER 2:2-5, NLT (EMPHASIS ADDED)

Notice that Peter doesn't say, "You are living stones that God has finished building into his spiritual temple"—no, God is *in the process* of building you. Still working on you. Still shaping you. Still making you into the woman he wants you to be.

We are called to grow into a full experience of salvation. Throughout your life, you will mature and leave some old habits and weaknesses behind, but God will never be finished with you. Even when you're a little old lady with veiny hands and silver hair, God will still be working in your heart—you will still need to grow!

The apostle Paul puts it this way:

Not that I have already obtained all this, or have already arrived at my goal, but I press on to take hold of that for which Christ Jesus took hold of me. Brothers and sisters, I do not consider myself yet to have taken hold of it. But one thing I do: Forgetting what is behind and straining toward what is ahead, I press on toward the goal to win the prize for which God has called me heavenward in Christ Jesus.

PHILIPPIANS 3:12-14

Even Paul, who had served Jesus for many years and had more Bible knowledge than you or I could ever hope to have, was still growing! He hadn't "arrived" spiritually. He didn't dwell on his past mistakes; he just kept his eyes focused on the person he was becoming in Christ.

START GIVING

One of my favorite things about Christianity is that we get to give. In Christ, our lives aren't just about us—what *we* want, what makes *us* happy. Our lives are about God, and they're about other people. Our lives mean something. With God working through us, we can help make the world a better place.

What emotional strengths have you identified in yourself as you have read? Our emotional gifts are like muscles. All muscles have potential, but if we don't exercise them, they stay weak and underdeveloped. But the more we use them, the stronger they grow and the more powerful they become.

Let's say you've discovered that you have emotional gifts of compassion and insight. How can you use those gifts at home with your family? At school with your friends? At church with your spiritual community? The more you put those gifts to work, the more they'll grow.

If you're a big feeler, can your joy lift others' spirits? Can your hope give others courage? Can your sensitivity help others to feel heard, known, and understood? Can your kindness bring positive change to your friends' lives?

If you're a steady feeler, can your consistent faith in God help your family stay faithful through difficulty? Can your stability help your more emotional friends stay strong? Can your compassionate problem-solving help others feel understood and helped at the same time?

If you're a reluctant feeler, can your calm attitude help others feel safe when crisis strikes? Can your clear-mindedness help panicky friends find God's will in life's storms? Can your peaceful, fair-minded spirit help friends and family members get along?

You have so much to give. When God made you, I picture him stepping back and whispering to Jesus, "Oh, this girl is good—she is very, very good. I can't wait to see what she does with all the gifts I gave her." So go ahead—start giving. Start using those gifts, building those emotional muscles. Step into the person God made you to be.

GOD GETS YOU

Our family is at Disney World, and the afternoon parade is about to start. We are surrounded by a swarm of strollers and sunburned people all decked out in Mickey Mouse everything. People are jostling for space at the front of the parade route, squeezing in close and spilling out into the street, like too many crayons jammed into a box.

My youngest, Sawyer, lifts her golden-brown eyes to me. She is four (*four* meaning "at the height of Princess Mania"), and today she is rocking her Arendelle finest: a long-sleeved, pale blue Princess Anna dress, complete with fake fur trim, and her hair in Anna braids. "Mommy, can we go see the parade?"

I hesitate. I'm not a big fan of so-close-you-can-feel-people-breathing-on-you crowds. "Oh, honey, the street is already so crowded. Why don't we go ride something right now? The lines will be short!"

Her eyes droop, disappointed.

Kevin studies her. "You want to see Anna, don't you?"

Sawyer nods.

"You want to show her your dress, don't you?"

Another nod.

Kevin looks at me. I know this look: it's his I'm-making-this-happen face. "Y'all stay here. We can do this." He sweeps a squealing-with-joy Sawyer into his arms and plunges into the crowd. I hang back with the stroller and the three older kids on a little bridge, where we can watch Kevin and Sawyer elbow their way through the crowd.

I shake my head in laughing awe: somehow Kevin finds a spot right in the front. He turns to give me a triumphant thumbs-up. A few minutes later, he starts bouncing on his tippy-toes and pointing wildly. I follow his finger. Sure enough, Elsa and Anna are coming! (You've never seen a grown man so ecstatic to see princesses in your life.)

He hoists Sawyer onto his shoulders, her blue dress billowing around his head. Sawyer hangs on to his neck, and he starts flinging his arms around like a maniac. His voice booms over the crowd. "Anna! Look! My daughter is you!"

As if in slow motion, Anna turns. Searches the hundreds of faces beneath the parade float. Spots Sawyer and Kevin. Grins and waves directly at them. But it gets even better: Anna squints at them more closely, then breaks into an even bigger grin. She points to Sawyer's dress, then down to her own, and calls out over the mayhem and music, "You're *me*! You look beautiful!"

Sawyer's smile is as big as Cinderella's castle.

Then I see Kevin. The joy on his face could power a hot-air balloon. He's flushed, he's laughing—as happy as I've ever seen him. Why? Because he just gave his daughter a priceless moment, a shining childhood memory.

I get teary eyed every time I think about those magical seconds—not just because they represent Kevin's love for his daughter, but because they also paint a picture in my mind of what it feels like to be a daughter of God. They remind me how much our Father loves to make our hearts happy—to swing us onto his strong shoulders when our legs get tired, to create a way to make us smile. He knows us—who we are, what we love, all the secret dreams we hold in our hearts and can't put into words. Of course, life isn't perfect, and it definitely won't feel like a Disney parade all the time. But our Father does want joy for us. And he carries us always and everywhere, no matter our circumstances.

As you head back out into the world, remember this: whether your life today feels like Disney World or a Pit of Doom, God is with you, and he understands your feelings—the wild ones, the weird ones, the ones you don't even have names for. He sent his own Son to live on earth—to become a human just like us—so that he would understand all we suffer, all we feel:

> Since we have a great High Priest who has entered heaven, Jesus the Son of God, let us hold firmly to what we believe. This High Priest of ours understands our weaknesses, for he faced all of the same testings we do, yet he did not sin. So let us come boldly to the throne of our gracious God. There we will receive his mercy, and we will find grace to help us when we need it most.
>
> HEBREWS 4:14-16, NLT

Do you understand what this means for us? Jesus came to earth and experienced all the feels, just like we do. The only difference (this teeny-tiny thing)? He never sinned (and of course it's not teeny-tiny at all). But God sent him here so he could better understand us—and so we would *know* he understands. So he could say, "I've felt that way too. I've been anxious like that. Lonely like that. Hurt like that."

And Jesus relates to every kind of feeler. Like a steady feeler, he felt intensely but had the courage, self-control, and determination to keep moving forward, to do the right thing. Like a reluctant feeler, Jesus didn't change his actions based on other people's opinions; he stuck to fairness and truth above all. Like a big feeler, he loved with his whole heart, and he gave everything he had to save his friends.

God is the Creator who breathed life and breath into us all, the Designer who crafted our personalities and feeling styles, the Friend who understands who we are, how we think, and how we feel. He is the Father of the reluctant feeler, the steady feeler, the big feeler, and every kind of feeler in between.

As simple as this sounds (and as hard as it can be to wrap your brain around), God likes you *so much*. You give him all the feels: all the happy, proud, protective feels. He is giddy over who you are and how he made you. He relishes watching you and helping you grow and feel and love:

> The LORD your God is living among you.
>> He is a mighty savior.
> He will take delight in you with gladness.
>> With his love, he will calm all your fears.
>> He will rejoice over you with joyful songs.
>
> ZEPHANIAH 3:17, NLT

Do you hear the love in these words? Can't you feel it—the kindness that forgives sins, the excitement that breaks into song, the affection that pulls you in for a big bear hug?

He delights in you, his darling girl.

You make him sing.

You.

Yes, you.

You, with all the feelings.

FEELING YOUR WAY FORWARD

Journal Prompts

1. How have you grown when it comes to your feelings while reading this book?
2. How would you like to grow moving forward?
3. Which aspects of your emotional life are you most excited about expanding?

Prayer Prompt

The LORD will work out his plans for my life—
    for your faithful love, O LORD, endures forever.
    Don't abandon me, for you made me.

PSALM 138:8, NLT

Lifelines

Five Scriptures about growth in Christ:

1. Ephesians 4:14-15
2. Philippians 1:3-6
3. 2 Corinthians 12:9-10
4. Hebrews 12:1-3
5. 1 John 2:28

ALL THE FEELS—TOGETHER!

Discussion Starters and Activities
for Mothers and Daughters, Mentors and Mentees

The only thing better than growing in your emotional life is growing closer to other people at the same time! This section offers ideas for conversations and activities you can do with a godly woman in your life: your mom, an aunt, a grandmother, or a spiritual mentor.

The idea is that they can read *All the Feels* (my book for adults) while you read *All the Feels for Teens*, and then you can talk about what you're learning together.

The discussions and activities are organized based on the chapters in *All the Feels for Teens*. There are a few different options for each chapter. You can choose whichever discussions and activities most appeal to you—make this your own!

I'm excited for you to grow together! Honored that you've chosen *All the Feels* and *All the Feels for Teens* to help you on that journey. Eager to hear how it's going. Thrilled, humbled, tickled pink . . . well, you know. All the feels.

CHAPTER 1: ALL THE FEELS, ALL THE TIME

Discussion Starters

1. How does it change your view of God when you think about him creating emotions and experiencing them himself?

2. Are there certain emotions you can easily picture God having and some that are hard to imagine him having? Which ones?

Activity

Test your knowledge of God's emotions by answering True or False to each of these statements:

1. God gets angry.
2. God experiences joy.
3. God feels grief.
4. God is afraid.
5. God feels proud of things he has done or made.
6. God wants to feel love from people.
7. God feels insecure.
8. God is jealous.
9. God can feel betrayed or rejected.
10. God feels compassion.

Now check out these Scriptures as you discuss whether the above statements are true or false:

1. 2 Chronicles 30:8; Psalm 86:15
2. Psalm 104:31; Zephaniah 3:17; Isaiah 65:19
3. Genesis 6:6
4. Isaiah 12:2, 41:14
5. Genesis 1:31
6. Matthew 23:37
7. Isaiah 44:7-8
8. Psalm 79:5
9. Jeremiah 3:19-20; Luke 22:48
10. Isaiah 49:13

CHAPTER 2: FINDING YOUR FEELING TYPE

Discussion Starters

Take the "What Kind of Feeler Are You?" quiz on page 20 together and determine what kind of feeler you are. Discuss these questions:

1. In what ways are you similar to each other in terms of your emotional makeup? How are you different?
2. How does your feeling type show itself in your life, your relationships, and your faith?
3. What's your favorite thing about your feeling type?

Activities

1. Scripture challenge: Pick an emotion to focus on, like anger, joy, peace, patience, or insecurity. Find as many verses as you can to address that emotion. Choose one passage to memorize together.
2. Help each other brainstorm some ways you can encourage someone using the gifts of your feeling type this week.

CHAPTER 3: WHEN FEELINGS TELL LIES

Discussion Starters

1. Discuss the "Myths about Feelings" chart in chapter 3.
2. Which myth (or myths) are you most often tempted to believe? Why?

Activities

1. Scripture challenge: Every day this week, choose one adjective from the Philippians 4:8 list as your theme for the day (true, noble, right, pure, etc.). When you think of or notice something that fits that adjective, send each other a text or picture describing it. At the end of the week, discuss how this activity affected your mood throughout the week.

2. Think about something you feel worried or upset about. Go through the acknowledge/assess/address or adiós process with that thought. What did you learn about your thought process through this exercise?

CHAPTER 4: WHO'S CALLING THE SHOTS?

Discussion Starters

1. Describe a time when you didn't want to follow God's ways but you chose to do the right thing anyway. What happened, and how did you feel in the end?
2. Now describe a time when you didn't want to follow God's ways and you didn't. How did that turn out?

Activity

Take a look at the "believe God" statements on page 47. Which of those statements do you find easiest to believe? Which are hardest to believe? Brainstorm a few more statements of your own to add to the list—truths you want to cling to instead of how you're feeling in any given moment.

CHAPTER 5: WHAT GOD HAS TO SAY TO YOU

Discussion Starters

1. What do you enjoy about reading the Bible? What do you find difficult or intimidating? Which parts of the Bible are easy for you to understand, and which are more difficult?
2. What questions do you have about faith or the Bible? What would you like to learn more about? What are some ways you could start learning about those things?
3. Share about a time when a Bible verse had a big impact on your heart.

Activities

1. Buy or make journals where you can both record lifeline verses as you find them. If you enjoy being crafty, decorate and personalize your journals together!
2. Scripture challenge: Share a Bible verse that has strengthened your faith or helped you through a difficult time. Memorize it and add it to your list of lifeline verses!

CHAPTER 6: HANDLING ALL THE FEELS AT HOME

Discussion Starters

1. This chapter describes three qualities we need to cultivate at home: selflessness, self-awareness, and self-control. Which of these qualities do you find easiest to embrace?
2. Which do you find more difficult? Why?

Activities

1. Take the "Big Feelings Check" quiz on page 68 and discuss your answers together.
2. Write down some of the warning signs that indicate your big feelings are getting the best of you. Do you . . .

   - get cranky?
   - distract yourself by becoming overly busy?
   - numb yourself with social media?
   - turn to comfort foods?
   - withdraw from other people?
   - become impatient and irritable?

   Share your warning signs with each other. How can you support each other when you notice that the other person's warning signs are going off?

3. Take another look at the chart on page 80 that shows you how to reframe dramatic thoughts. Now use the chart on this page to write down some thoughts you've had recently and reframe them according to God's perspective.

A DRAMATIC THOUGHT YOU STRUGGLE WITH:	REFRAME THAT THOUGHT IN A MORE GODLY OR REALISTIC WAY:	A SCRIPTURE THAT BACKS UP YOUR NEW THOUGHT:

CHAPTER 7: HOW GOD FEELS ABOUT YOU
Discussion Starters

1. Where does your view of yourself come from? How did reading this chapter change the way you think about yourself?
2. How do you think God feels about you? Which of these statements is easiest for you to believe, and which is most difficult? Why?

   - You are blameless.
   - You are never forgotten.
   - You are forgiven.
   - You are understood and known.
   - You are God's beloved child.

Activities

1. Find a few Scriptures that describe God's feelings toward you and add them to your list of lifeline verses. Pick one to discuss or memorize together.
2. Choose a verse that talks about the way God sees you. Now get crafty together! Print out your verse in a pretty font, or get out your favorite colored pencils or markers and write the passage by hand. (You can find fun, free calligraphy tutorials online!) Tape the verse to your mirror this week to remind you of your true identity.

CHAPTER 8: WHEN YOU CAN'T DEAL
Discussion Starters

1. Take the "How Drama Prone Are You?" quiz on page 107 and discuss what you learned about yourself.

2. Describe a time when you were anxious and God took care of you. How specifically did he take care of you? Did he . . .

- provide a friend to support you?
- help you find a solution to a problem?
- give you strength and courage?

3. As you remember the care and faithfulness God has already shown you, how does that change the way you view your current problems and worries?

Activities

1. Write down something you are each feeling overwhelmed about. Then go through the six strategies for dealing with overwhelming feelings together.
2. Take time this week to text encouraging Scriptures to each other about trusting God and embracing peace.
3. Find a Bible verse that describes how powerful and capable God is in caring for you. Memorize it and add it to your list of lifeline verses.

CHAPTER 9: WHEN FEELINGS CRASH THE FRIENDSHIP PARTY

Discussion Starters

1. Describe the qualities you'd want in an ideal friend.
2. Which friendship myth(s) do you wrestle with? Why do you think people buy into this misconception?
3. Which friendship blocker do you struggle with the most? Which friendship booster do you want to add into your life?

Activities

1. Take "The Friendship Checkup" quiz on page 126 and discuss your answers together.
2. Do something fun together this week!
3. What is going well in your friendships? What do you wish were different? Pray together about those things.

CHAPTER 10: PRAYING THROUGH ALL YOUR EMOTIONS

Discussion Starters

1. How do you feel about your prayer life? What do you enjoy about prayer?
2. Does any aspect of prayer feel uncomfortable, awkward, or intimidating? What would you like your prayer life to feel like?

Activities

1. Try out one of the "ways to pray" together and then talk about it afterward. What did you think of the experience?
2. Create a worship playlist together! Come up with a list of worship songs that help you both to connect with God emotionally, and share your playlist.

CHAPTER 11: WHEN GUILT COMES KNOCKING

Discussion Starters

1. How often do you struggle with feelings of guilt? What did you learn from this chapter that might help you when you feel guilty?
2. How can you tell the difference between phantom guilt and legitimate guilt?

Activities

1. Pay attention to little encouragements God sends you each day to show you his love (a nice text from a friend, a homework-free night, even getting that parking space you prayed for!). Spend a week writing down these things every day, then share your list with each other. Spend some time together thanking God for his gifts!

2. Scripture challenge: What's your favorite Scripture about grace, and why? Talk about it or memorize it, and add it to your lifeline list!

CHAPTER 12: ALL THE SWOONS

Discussion Starters

1. Ask your mom or mentor to share about one of their middle or high school crushes or boyfriends. If they were to do it over again, would they do anything differently?

2. Talk about where you are with dating. Are you ready to date yet? Why or why not? What are some guidelines you'd like to establish in your relationships/interactions with guys? If you're making decisions about whether to date a particular boy, talk through the sidebar lists/questions together.

Activity

Scripture challenge: Find a Bible verse that makes you feel loved by God. Write it down or memorize it, and add it to your lifeline list.

CHAPTER 13: SOCIAL MEDIA: THE GOOD, THE BAD, AND THE AIRBRUSHED

Discussion Starters

1. Read Colossians 3:1-2 together:

   > Set your hearts on things above, where Christ is,
   > seated at the right hand of God. Set your minds
   > on things above, not on earthly things.

   What earthly things tend to take up a lot of your thoughts?
   What are some godly things you can focus on? How can
   you set your mind more on things above?

2. How does social media affect you? How would you
   describe its influence on your faith? Your relationships?
   Your spiritual and emotional health?

Activities

1. Take the social media quizzes on pages 178–179 and
   discuss your results. What did you both learn about
   yourselves?
2. Scripture challenge: Find a Bible verse that you want to
   guide your words and actions on social media. Talk about
   it or memorize it, and add it to your lifeline list!

CHAPTER 14: WHERE DO WE GO FROM HERE?

Discussion Starters

1. Encourage the other person by describing some ways you've
   seen them grow as they've read this book.
2. Discuss the journal prompts at the end of the chapter
   together.

Activities

1. Pray together about what you've learned and how you'd like to use your emotional gifts moving forward.

2. Find or make a memento to mark your journey together. Look through your own stuff and find something that reminds you of the other person's personality and feeling-type gifts. Maybe it's a piece of jewelry or a book or a piece of artwork. Give it to them as a memento of your time together. If you like being crafty, you could make this a craft challenge instead. Get out a bunch of art supplies and make each other something (a bookmark, a painting, a drawing, a card, a bracelet) as a reminder of the moments you've shared.

3. Go out for ice cream or cake or coffee or tea (or whatever floats your taste-bud boat!) to celebrate the time you've spent growing together in your faith and feelings.

ACKNOWLEDGMENTS

I am infinitely grateful to God for allowing me the privilege of writing this book. The whole reason I got into writing in the first place was so I could write for my favorite humans—tween and teen girls—and what a thrill it was to write this book. Thank you, Father, for your constant presence, guidance, and inspiration—how I love writing with you.

I owe an indescribable debt to my family for their support during the writing of this book. Kevin, only you fully know what a doozy this year was. Thank you for never flinching and always believing. Praise God we made it through! And we still really like each other! Ha! My kids, Cassidy, Blake, Avery, and Sawyer, were tremendously generous in sharing me with multiple books this past year—and all this during a pandemic and remote school. Thank you for being flexible, resilient, joyful, and just so stinkin' delightful. You make me happier—and prouder—than I can say.

Mom and Dad, when God packed all these big feelings inside me, he knew it was going to take some astoundingly wise and patient parents to help me figure out how to deal and grow and thrive. I'm forever and ever thankful he gave me you. Thank you for every talk, every laugh, every hug, every reassurance that the way I felt was normal and that it was all going to be okay. You were infinitely patient, with impressive skills at making no-we're-not-freaked-out-by-your-huge-feelings faces, and I am too-big-for-words grateful.

My in-laws achieved Superhero Status during the writing of this book. I couldn't possibly list all the ways you supported our family during The Year of COVID-19 and Multiple Deadlines and Launches, but please know how grateful I am. We couldn't have made it without you.

To my writing partner, Emma Stephens: THANK YOU. (That was me shouting all the way to Georgia.) Your heart for teens and your giftedness as both a teacher and a writer were invaluable in guiding this book. You gave countless hours to reading and critiquing during a hectic time in your own life, and I am forever grateful. Thank you for shaping this book (and me!) in more ways than I can say.

Ginormous thanks go to all the girls on my teen advisory panel (how do you like the fancy name?!), who Zoomed with me and gave me ideas and insights as I was preparing to write. Hearing your stories and your heart for God was an absolute joy and inspiration. Thank you, Cassidy, Isabelle, Rebekah, Reese, Chloe, Lily, Kayli, Ariana, and Gabriela, for sharing your hearts, your stories, and your ideas.

Thank you to the Anchor girls—Rosa, Elisabeth, Ashleigh, Gigi, and Cassidy—for sharing your hearts for God with me! Spending time with you every Wednesday is a highlight of my week.

Endless thanks go to Jessie Kirkland, my agent, who retired as I was finishing this book. We started working together five years ago with dreams of touching girls' hearts—look what God is letting us do now! Working with you changed my life—thank you for *everything*.

The staff at Tyndale Kids/Wander has made this labor of love a labor of *joy*! Stephanie Rische, you are a dream. Your intuition, insight, heart, sensitivity, depth of scriptural understanding, and sense of humor have influenced every page—indeed, every line—of this book. This book is infinitely better because of your gifted editing, compassionate encouragement, and genuine friendship—thank you from the bottom of my big-feeling heart.

Thank you to Linda Howard for believing in this project from the get-go, and then keeping all the wheels turning and plates spinning to make it the best book it could be . . . and all this through a pandemic!

Libby Dykstra, the cover is ah-mazing! I stand in awe of your design talents. I couldn't love it more.

Special thanks to copyediting coordinator Debbie King—thank you for stepping in with your awesomeness when we needed you! Huge shout-outs and hugs to Kristi Gravemann and Annette Taroli for all you have done to usher this book into the world and help it find its place. Alyssa Clements, thank you for working your wonders, keeping so many things running—sometimes when no one could see all you were doing, like a super-spy secret agent we can't live without.

ABOUT THE AUTHOR

ELIZABETH LAING THOMPSON wrote her first story when she was five, and she's been writing ever since. She met the dashing man who became her husband when they were both in high school—though it was years before they dated. It took her going out on a date with another guy—in Paris, of all places—to make Kevin realize that she wasn't going to sit around being his best friend forever. Elizabeth and Kevin have spent most of their married life serving God in campus ministries all across the Southeast, and eight years ago, they planted a church in a midsize beach town. After nearly three years of trying to start a family, she and Kevin had their first baby, born on Christmas Day—the greatest gift they've ever received. More babies came along—one boy and two girls. Now they live on the North Carolina coast with four spunky kids and a dog that thinks he's human. Kevin preaches, Elizabeth writes, and they both work with their church's youth ministry.

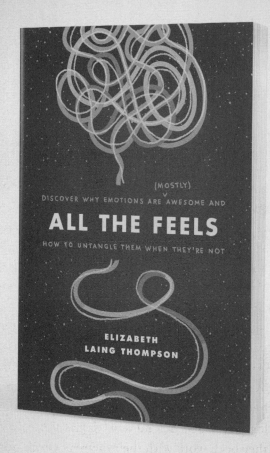

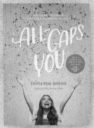